Praise for *SEL Fr*

"Jessica and John Hannigan have written an immensely valuable and timely resource for educators to help them better understand the social and emotional learning needs of the students they serve. The global pandemic has exacerbated the need for quality SEL instruction in the United States and across the world. This book is a 'call to action, not through compliance, but compassion.' With its many practical and essential tools, I recommend it to all educators for supporting their students during this consequential time."

Joseph I. Castro, President and
Professor of Educational Leadership
California State University, Fresno

"*SEL From a Distance* is a must-read guide that offers a message of hope during this unprecedented time in education, calling for the intentional teaching and designing of essential SEL skills necessary for success in school and real life. I highly recommend this book for any educator looking to improve students' relationship, responsible decision making, social awareness, self-management, or self-awareness skills."

Karen DeOrian, Director of School Culture and Climate
Madera Unified School District, CA

"Of all the topics I write about for my Finding Common Ground Blog (*Education Week*), social and emotional learning is the one where I get the most pushback from readers. Time, and the feeling that that SEL is the job of parents or school leaders, are often seen as the biggest roadblocks to focusing on it. Finally, due to COVID-19, people are seeing the importance of SEL, and Jessica Hannigan and John Hannigan have written a timely and responsive book that will help teachers and leaders create opportunities for students to become more independent and successful now, during distance learning, and in the future."

Peter DeWitt, Author/Blogger/Consultant

"With the rise in anxiety, depression, and suicide over the last few years, schools have faced the challenge of how to address the social and emotional needs of all students. Now, during the pandemic, the need is more acute and schools require more assistance. *SEL From a Distance* offers an easy-to-follow framework to build our students' skills in the key SEL competencies. The authors have taken a complex topic and created an easy-to-use guide for school teams and leaders. Any school searching for what to do next should pick up this book."

Brian Jaramillo, Executive Director of Education Services
Lompoc Unified School District, CA

"Social and emotional learning is a crucial component of student/child development and life functioning. Jessica and John Hannigan have created a resource that addresses the need for SEL instruction for all our students and provides relevant supports for immediate use and application. I will certainly keep this book at the edge of my bookshelf for frequent reference!"

Dr. Sarah Marriott, Superintendent of Schools
Boonville R-1 School District, MO

"For many years our district has provided professional development for our administrators, teachers, and classified staff on social and emotional learning. COVID-19 has brought the critical need of SEL to the forefront of educators' thinking, because now many have experienced trauma in their own lives. *SEL From a Distance* is grounded in research yet so practical that all educators should have it in their hands."

Andrea Morici, Director of Professional Development
Paradise Valley Unified School District, AZ

"What is great about this book is that it provides a clear process to identify students' needs followed by effective and practical methods to teach these critical social and emotional skills. The learning and support students receive will help them at school, at home, and within their communities for the rest of their lives. The book does an excellent job of supporting educators in an area where we often struggle and need additional support."

Eduardo Ochoa, Assistant Superintendent
Lemoore Union Elementary School District, CA

"Once again, Jessica and John Hannigan have created a fantastic resource for educators! *SEL From a Distance* takes a complex concept, social and emotional distance learning, and makes it incredibly easy to understand and put into practice. At a time when many educators are teaching from a distance and the need for social and emotional learning and support has escalated to previously unknown heights, this book will guide educators to overcome the challenges."

Heath Peine, Executive Director
Wichita Public Schools, KS

"Many educators are struggling to find a way to build relationships with students and teach them the social and emotional skills they are lacking via distance learning, and this book solves that problem. It is structured so that the reader and school teams can implement the techniques and strategies to best meet the needs of their students. The rubrics and activities can be easily implemented into core curriculum content across all grade levels.

I highly recommend this book for all school staff, support staff, and district office personnel to truly understand how to implement SEL in a concrete and appropriate way to ensure student success."

Brooke Warkentin, Director of Special Services
Lemoore Union Elementary School District, CA

PRAISE FROM STUDENTS

"My teacher told our class, 'If you need someone to talk to, I am here for you.' This was powerful to hear. I have never had a teacher say that to an entire class before."

Ani, 12th Grade, MO

"I love learning about my teacher and classmates. It has helped me see how much I have in common with other students."

Celia, 8th Grade, NY

"I love it when my teacher helps us learn how to stay organized with reminders and check-ins."

Darwin, 3rd Grade, CO

"My teacher helps us use strategies to relax our brains when we are feeling stressed."

Harmon, 4th Grade, CA

"Taking the time to say 'welcome' and 'good morning' to each student makes a huge difference in our day."

James, 5th Grade, AZ

"My teacher helps us learn how to problem solve as a classroom community."

Jaivon, 6th Grade, KS

"I like it when my teacher stays after the class session and answers questions."

Shay, 11th Grade, WY

This book is dedicated to all the educators who have abruptly adapted to events occurring as we wrote this book, including a pandemic and a spotlight on racial injustice, and who continue to work tirelessly to support students' social and emotional needs. We appreciate you all.

Jessica Djabrayan Hannigan ▪ John E. Hannigan

SEL FROM A DISTANCE

Tools and Processes for Anytime, Anywhere

CORWIN

FOR INFORMATION:

Corwin

A SAGE Company

2455 Teller Road

Thousand Oaks, California 91320

(800) 233-9936

www.corwin.com

SAGE Publications Ltd.

1 Oliver's Yard

55 City Road

London EC1Y 1SP

United Kingdom

SAGE Publications India Pvt. Ltd.

B 1/I 1 Mohan Cooperative Industrial Area

Mathura Road, New Delhi 110 044

India

SAGE Publications Asia-Pacific Pte. Ltd.

18 Cross Street #10-10/11/12

China Square Central

Singapore 048423

Publisher: Jessica Allan

Senior Content
    Development Editor: Lucas Schleicher

Associate Content
    Development Editor: Mia Rodriguez

Production Editor: Melanie Birdsall

Copy Editor: Lana Todorovic-Arndt

Typesetter: C&M Digitals (P) Ltd.

Proofreader: Sarah J. Duffy

Cover Designer: Rose Storey

Marketing Manager: Olivia Bartlett

Chapter-opening icons courtesy of istock.com/-VICTOR-.

Printed in the United States of America

ISBN 9781071840016

Library of Congress Control Number: 2020917771

This book is printed on acid-free paper.

21 22 23 24 10 9 8 7 6 5 4 3 2

CONTENTS

Visit the companion website at
resources.corwin.com/selfromadistance
for downloadable resources.

ABOUT THE AUTHORS

Dr. Jessica Djabrayan Hannigan is an assistant professor in the Educational Leadership Department at California State University, Fresno. She works with schools and districts across the nation on designing and implementing effective behavior systems. Her expertise includes response-to-intervention (RTI) behavior, multi-tiered systems of supports (MTSS), positive behavior interventions and supports (PBIS), social and emotional learning (SEL), and more. The combination of her background in special education and student support services, school- and district-level administration, and higher education research experiences has allowed her to develop inclusive research-based best practices around systemic implementation of behavior initiatives throughout the nation. Some of her achievements include being named California Outstanding School Psychologist of the Year and Administrator of the Year. In addition, she is an Outstanding Faculty Publications and Service Award recipient, being recognized by the California legislature for her work in social justice and equity, and receiving the inaugural Association of California School Administrators Exemplary Woman in Education Award in 2017 for her relentless work around equity in schools.

John E. Hannigan, EdD, is an executive leadership coach for Fresno County Superintendent of Schools in California. He has served in education for over 15 years as a principal, assistant principal, instructional coach, and teacher. Under his leadership, his school has received numerous awards and recognitions, including California State Distinguished School, Gold Ribbon School, Title I Academic School, Positive Behavioral Interventions and Supports (Platinum Level). In addition, it was recognized as an exemplary RTI school for both academics and behavior, and selected as a knowledge development site for the statewide scaling up of the MTSS.

PART **1**

THE WHAT AND WHY OF SEL

SEL is not just a curriculum; *it is the intentional teaching and design of a classroom environment with conditions and supports set up for real-life application and mastery of essential SEL skills necessary for success in school and beyond.*

WHY SEL IS MORE IMPORTANT NOW THAN EVER

The coronavirus disease of 2019 (COVID-19) pandemic has caused a great deal of reflection in our home. We have a 2020 high school graduate, a ninth grader, and a 3-year-old in our family—we have experienced firsthand the social and emotional impact that the abrupt transition to distance learning along with other significant life changes has had on our own children and the students we serve. As you are aware, in our schools, there were already significant mental health, social, emotional, and behavioral needs before the pandemic. For example, according to research over the past several decades (e.g., Centers for Disease Control and Prevention [CDC], 2020; CDC & Kaiser Permanente, 2016; Mojtabai, Olfson, & Han, 2016; National Institute of Mental

Health, 2018; Saeki et al., 2011; Skiba & Rauch, 2006; U.S. Department of Education, 2014; Visser et al., 2014):

- One in five children has mental health problems.
- There has been a 43% increase in attention-deficit/hyperactivity disorder cases (6.4 million children).
- There has been a 37% increase in teen depression nationwide.
- There has been a 100% increase in suicide rate in kids 10–14 years old.
- Sixty-four percent of students have experienced trauma, including witnessing violence and being direct targets of abuse.
- Educators struggle to address the increasing number of students who have social, emotional, and behavioral difficulties.
- There is a disproportionate amount of time spent serving a small number of students with social, emotional, and behavioral difficulties.
- Schools commonly address social, emotional, and behavioral difficulties with exclusionary practices such as detention, suspension, and expulsion.

Thus, social and emotional learning (SEL) has been part of education for decades. It certainly isn't a new topic; however, we are seeing it affect our students in historic ways. Moreover, we are seeing the *need* for it in historic ways. Consider just a few developing statistics during the COVID-19 period by National 4-H Council and the Harris Poll (2020) and EdWeek Research Center Survey (Harold & Kurtz, 2020):

- Seven out of 10 teens reported struggling with mental health in some way.
- More than half of the students surveyed experienced anxiety.
- Forty-five percent felt excessive stress.
- Forty-three percent identified as struggling with depression.
- Sixty-one percent reported loneliness.

- Compared to their engagement level prior to the COVID-19 closures, students' current level of engagement with their schoolwork has decreased significantly.
- One out of four students was reported to be essentially truant during the COVID-19 closures: MIA, not logging in, not making contact, etc.

The gaps have widened, and the cracks in the system in how we support SEL are no longer hidden in the traditional chaos of school. We have some students who may need additional support, some who did not need any prior to the pandemic but who do now, and some who just need to know they are loved and cared for. Essentially, it has become clear that SEL competencies—students having the strategies and real-life skills they need to be successful during this time—is the main focus of schools and districts around the nation and world.

Before the pandemic, the adults on campus (i.e., teachers, administration, staff) would see our students act out and respond to their misbehavior in the form of frustration or punishment. Very rarely would we view a student acting out as the result of the absence of a skill—for example, blurting out in class and showing a lack of self-control or self-awareness—and approach that student with the same compassion as if they were lacking an academic skill, such as detecting vowel blends and digraphs, impeding reading fluency. Typically, the absence of social and emotional skills is much more frustrating and difficult to manage than the absence of academic skills.

Education is at a crossroads, much like it was in the late 1990s to early 2000s with English learner development (ELD) instruction. English learners (ELs) faced the unique challenge of acquiring a new language while they were also learning grade-level content *through* English. The ELD was mostly served through "pull-out" sessions of anywhere from 30–90 minutes a day, and the Reading Recovery teacher in the "language lab" was responsible for developing and teaching language acquisition skills, while the responsibility rested on someone else in the building to serve these students' needs. We see a parallel in the way a student who struggles today with social and emotional skills is being "pulled out," and a school counselor or behavior specialist is responsible for developing and teaching social and emotional skills. In the early 2000s, concern began to grow about meeting the needs of the nation's growing population of ELs, driven in part by the No Child Left Behind (NCLB) accountability measures in the form of Adequate Yearly Progress (AYP) targets for the EL subgroup. We knew that specific population was struggling, and we were required to act. Today, we see the same call to action, not through compliance, but compassion. Our apathy toward teaching SEL has shifted to empathy—we the adults during this time have had the same feelings of anxiety, depression, excessive stress, and need for self-care as our students. We gave grace because we expected grace from the parents and administrators who understood that we, too, were learning how to teach through an unfamiliar platform. This pandemic, in part, has exacerbated the need for SEL instruction the same way NCLB exposed the extent to which our ELs were falling behind in learning.

This book wasn't written to be opportunistic or to attempt to capitalize on a moment. It is a call to arms. SEL support has been the highest need/request from schools we work with across the country. Hence, this book is a collection of support that we have been providing in schools since the pandemic hit.

We wrote this book to help educators successfully ease SEL into virtual, blended, hybrid, or in-person learning environments. When you apply the tools and processes highlighted in this book from a distance, you can most certainly apply them in any other learning environments. We also understand how overwhelming it feels to add SEL to your proverbial "teaching plate," so we will present the essential SEL competencies in a way that is easy to digest and quickly apply in your learning environment. We are not advocating against prepackaged SEL curricula, but rather advocating for a *process* to identify what skills our students are lacking and to teach, model, and reinforce those skills to reduce or eliminate the challenging behaviors you are witnessing. The SEL application needs to match the needs of your learning environment, whether in-person or virtual, based on current behavior data and not merely simplified into a predetermined list of topic areas for each month. We will provide you with easy-to-implement tools and processes that you can use immediately.

Educators will leave with a practical, easy-to-use toolkit of tools and processes to embed the most common social and emotional learning competencies into your virtual classrooms and schools. However, before we delve into the tools and processes, let's make sure we are grounded in some SEL common language.

Take a few minutes to complete this SEL common definition pre-check. Revisit and add to this pre-check after you read Chapter 2.

SEL Pre-Check
Define SEL.
List the SEL core competencies.
What is the purpose of implementing SEL?
List different ways/modalities SEL can be taught from a distance.

DIGGING INTO SEL

What Is SEL?

Simply put, social and emotional learning (SEL) is a structure designed to help students understand the relationship between emotions and behaviors in relation to their own self-worth, academic achievement, well-being, and ability to learn how to self-regulate and connect with others. However, there are some noteworthy variations in common SEL definitions and styles of implementation. Still, the intended outcomes for SEL implementation are similar.

What SEL Common Language Will Be Utilized for This Book?

We appreciate the research and work behind the Collaborative for Academic, Social, and Emotional Learning's (CASEL) definition and framework of SEL. Thus, for the purpose of this book, we will define SEL as follows: "Social and emotional learning enhances students' capacity to integrate skills, attitudes, and behaviors to deal effectively and ethically with daily tasks and challenges." CASEL's integrated framework promotes intrapersonal, inter-personal, and cognitive competence. There are five core compe-tencies that can be taught in many ways across many settings. The five core SEL competencies for which we will provide tools, processes, and strategies are Relationships Skills, Responsible Decision Making, Social Awareness, Self-Management, and Self-Awareness. We also want to note that we would like to deconstruct mastery by the sub-skill mastery descriptors per the following chart for each competency.

Five Core SEL Competencies	
	Relationship Skills (i.e., communication, social engagement, relationship building, teamwork)
	Responsible Decision Making (i.e., identifying problems, analyzing situations, solving problems, evaluation, reflecting, ethical responsibility)
	Social Awareness (i.e., perspective taking, empathy, appreciating diversity, respect for others)
	Self-Management (i.e., impulse control, stress management, self-discipline, self-motivation, goal setting, organizational skills)
	Self-Awareness (i.e., identifying emotions, accurate self-perception, recognizing strengths, self-confidence, self-efficacy)

Source: Five core SEL competencies from CASEL, https://casel.org/core-competencies. *Images source:* istock.com/-VICTOR-.

Why Implement SEL?

- ☐ Creates a climate and culture conducive to learning
- ☐ Integrates social and emotional skills into teaching practices such as cooperative and project-based learning
- ☐ Integrates social and emotional skills across academic curricula
- ☐ Improves achievement
- ☐ Improves resiliency skills
- ☐ Develops students' self-awareness and self-management skills that are essential in school and life
- ☐ Demonstrates ethical decision-making skills in personal, school, and community contexts
- ☐ Improves student connectedness
- ☐ Improves student learning
- ☐ Increases prosocial behaviors
- ☐ Improves students' attitudes toward school
- ☐ Reduces depression and stress among students
- ☐ Improves mental health
- ☐ Improves social skills

Why SEL Now More Than Ever?

Students need to learn and apply these social and emotional skills now more than ever.

- ☐ Increase in mental health needs
- ☐ Increase in number of students with depression
- ☐ Increase in number of students with anxiety
- ☐ Increase in number of students feeling excessive stress
- ☐ Increase in number of students who are experiencing or witnessing trauma (adverse childhood experiences)
- ☐ Increase in number of students reporting loneliness
- ☐ Increase in suicide rate
- ☐ Increase in disengagement

(Continued)

(Continued)

☐ Increase in truancy

☐ Need to build resiliency in students

☐ Need for emotional safety

☐ Need for physical safety

☐ Need for relationships and connections

SEL Imagery

We also want to provide you with a quick imagery exercise to reflect on your current state of SEL integration and your future desired state. Imagine this for a few minutes:

SEL integration before distance learning . . . some educators struggled to understand the importance of integrating SEL in their classrooms. They struggled with the idea of having one more thing added to their already packed schedules of teaching academic content. Some felt it was the parent's job to teach students these skills and not something taught at school. Many others were given an SEL curriculum with minimal training and asked to consistently implement it based on an arbitrary schedule (30 minutes per week) that may or may not be monitored with student data. Some viewed SEL as mindfulness or deep-breathing activities. Nonetheless, teachers were sharing concerns about an absence of students' social and emotional skills, and they were overwhelmed with adding SEL to their plate as another responsibility. More specifically, they did not feel appropriate training and tools were provided to implement SEL in a meaningful way.

SEL integration during distance learning . . . teachers realized the impact of trauma and crisis on themselves and students' social and emotional well-being. They realized the importance of being adaptable and intentionally teaching students how to be resilient in any learning setting and in real life. It quickly became apparent that learning could not exist if students did not feel safe and welcomed and possess the skills needed to be successful and persistent. Simply put, they realized they had to go back to Maslow's basics before any learning would occur. However, many educators continued to struggle with meaningful ways to teach and model SEL from a distance. Most were required to teach only SEL (and turn in lesson plans as evidence) for the first 3 weeks of school; however, the response and implementation was not designed to meet actual student needs. In addition, the mandatory implementation of 45 minutes a day for 3 weeks led to compliance rather than collective, ongoing ownership and priority of this work.

Briefly state your feelings and perceptions about your roll-out of SEL from a distance (or current status) at this time:

_____

_____

_____

_____

Imagine your desired state. What would you want this to look like and feel like for you and your students? Take a minute to write down a few sentences now.

_____

_____

_____

_____

Next, we are going to walk you through how to be best prepared to get the maximum impact from the tools and processes around each SEL competency section in this book.

Behaviors vs. Skills

Take a moment and ask yourself: (1) What are the challenging student *behaviors* you are seeing? Then, for each challenging behavior listed, ask yourself: (2) What SEL *skill* is the student lacking (i.e., what skill needs to be taught and modeled for the student to not engage in each challenging behavior)?

1. What are the challenging student *behaviors* you are seeing?	2. What SEL *skill* is the student lacking (i.e., what skill needs to be taught and modeled for the student to not engage in each challenging behavior)?

Unless you left both columns blank, there is a need for this SEL work!

The following is a sample from a school team using this process to help reframe their thinking about the identified challenging behavior.

Note: Although we provided a sample here, it does not mean that the SEL skill we identified with each behavior is the only one that fits. Knowing your students by name and by need will help you identify the function or the skill they may be lacking.

1. What are the challenging student *behaviors* you are seeing?	2. What SEL *skill* is the student lacking (i.e., what skill needs to be taught and modeled for the student to not engage in each challenging behavior)?
Apathy	Social awareness
Lack of engagement	Self-discipline
Silent	Self-confidence
Disruptive	Impulse control
Lack of focus	Goal setting
Opposition	Solving problems
Attention seeking	Relationship building
Peer attention	Social engagement
Shutting down	Identifying emotions
Lack of motivation	Self-motivation
Anger	Stress management
Staying organized	Organization
Giving up easily	Self-efficacy

The purpose of walking you through this exercise is to provide a new way of thinking about and reframing the challenging behaviors you are seeing in your classrooms. When reframed in this way, you will identify the appropriate SEL skills students need intentionally taught to them. SEL skills aren't cultivated through genetics: They need to be taught as a matter of course. Our students come into our classrooms as the product of the best version of these skills developed over the course of their lives up to this very moment. When they come to us with SEL gaps, we need to diagnose these gaps as skills missing and teach those skills in the same way we would fill academic gaps in learning, specifically in the way we did for designated and integrated systematic ELD instruction as a result of NCLB.

Note: Teaching SEL skills takes time and patience. In addition, our students' brains develop and learn these skills well into their mid-20s. This does not happen in the same fashion and time span for all students. They need multiple opportunities in a variety of modalities to learn these skills and apply (generalize) them for true SEL to occur. Take a few minutes to read through the lists that follow to begin the calibration of your thinking between skill and behavior.

SEL Competency (Skill) to Behavior Observed Calibration	
SEL Competency (skill)	**Absence of skill could look like (behaviors) . . .**
Relationship Skills	Student struggles to make or keep friends. Student struggles with communicating with others. Student has difficulty working with others. Student struggles with working in teams. Student has difficulty with reading social cues. Some examples may be • Gossips (starts rumors) • Online bullying • Makes fun of peers
Responsible Decision Making	Student struggles with making appropriate decisions. Student struggles with understanding the difference between wrong and right. Student struggles to think through their decisions before engaging in a behavior or speaks out loud. Some examples may be • Blurts out • Interrupts teacher or other students • Makes inappropriate comments in chats and assignments
Social Awareness	Student struggles to see another person's point of view. Student struggles with positive interactions with adults and peers. Student struggles with recognizing diversity. Student struggles with problem-solving peacefully. Some examples may be • Argues with others • Talks back • Makes inappropriate comments

SEL Competency (skill)	Absence of skill could look like (behaviors) . . .
Self-Management	Student struggles with staying on task. Student struggles with being organized. Student struggles with motivation. Student struggles to control emotions. Some examples may be • Curses • Appears tired • Acts out • Gives up easily
Self-Awareness	Student struggles with their emotions and responses. Student struggles with self-monitoring emotions. Student struggles with self-esteem. Some examples may be • Cries easily • Leaves the in-person or virtual classroom • Takes a long time to calm down when they are upset

Images source: istock.com/-VICTOR-.

Now that you have begun to think about skills and behaviors in this way, we want to introduce you to our SEL Competency Implementation Framework.

SEL Competency Implementation Framework

The SEL Competency Implementation Framework requires the use of data and stakeholder input to develop, implement, and adjust as needed, based on responses to the SEL competency needs of the students.

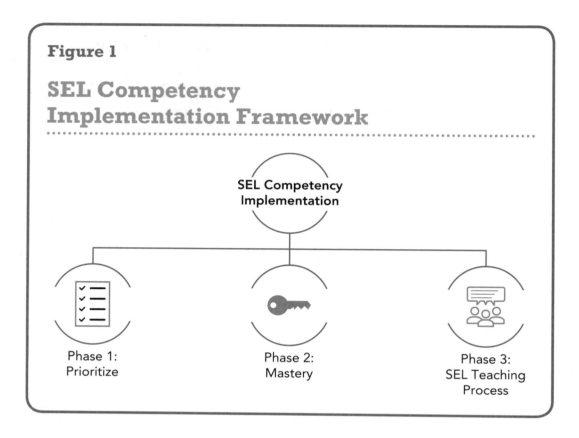

Figure 1

SEL Competency Implementation Framework

SEL Competency Implementation

Phase 1: Prioritize

Phase 2: Mastery

Phase 3: SEL Teaching Process

The Framework is divided into three phases and is designed to help teachers, teacher teams, and schools through effective SEL implementation:

- **Phase 1: Prioritize**. Prioritize the SEL competency and related skill(s) of focus based on data and stakeholder input and needs.

- **Phase 2: Mastery**. Develop a rubric for mastery of the priority SEL competency and related skill(s) of focus based on data and evidence indicators.

- **Phase 3: SEL Teaching Process**. Embed the priority SEL competency and related skill(s) into the SEL Teaching Process: identify, teach, model, and reinforce.

PHASE 1: PRIORITIZE

Prioritize the SEL competency and related skill(s) of focus based on data and stakeholder input and needs.

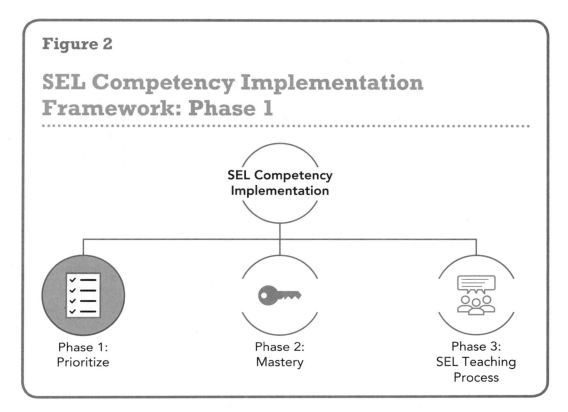

Figure 2

SEL Competency Implementation Framework: Phase 1

SEL Competency Implementation

Phase 1:
Prioritize

Phase 2:
Mastery

Phase 3:
SEL Teaching
Process

What Happens in the Prioritize Phase?

First, complete the SEL Competency Priority Forced Rating Scale to focus your efforts in a way that is going to be the most effective for your students.

The SEL Competency Priority Forced Rating Scale is designed to help educators identify and prioritize the SEL competencies they will be teaching based on student grade level, learning environment, and department need. Although this tool is designed to help educators prioritize, it does not mean the comprehensive list of SEL competencies and deconstructed skills are not essential for students to learn.

Steps to the Process

- Each team member is given an unranked list of items and criteria for ranking them.
- When team members are finished ranking independently, tally up the rankings for the SEL competency list.
- Discuss and get consensus on highest priority. *The lowest total, the highest priority.*

Competencies will likely vary depending on the grade level of the students.

Date: _____

Team or individual completing rating scale: _____

TM = team member

SEL Competency	TM1	TM2	TM3	TM4	Overall rank order score (1 "highest priority"–5 "lowest priority")
Relationship Skills (i.e., communication, social engagement, relationship building, teamwork)					
Responsible Decision Making (i.e., identifying problems, analyzing situations, solving problems, evaluation, reflecting, ethical responsibility)					
Social Awareness (i.e., perspective taking, empathy, appreciating diversity, respect for others)					
Self-Management (i.e., impulse control, stress management, self-discipline, self-motivation, goal setting, organizational skills)					
Self-Awareness (i.e., identifying emotions, accurate self-perception, recognizing strengths, self-confidence, self-efficacy)					
Highest priority SEL competency:					

PHASE 2: MASTERY

Develop a rubric for mastery of the priority SEL competency and related skill(s) of focus based on data and evidence indicators.

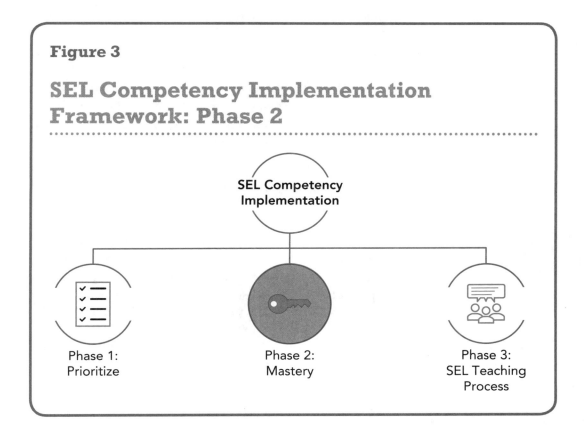

Figure 3

SEL Competency Implementation Framework: Phase 2

SEL Competency Implementation

Phase 1: Prioritize

Phase 2: Mastery

Phase 3: SEL Teaching Process

What Happens in the Mastery Phase?

You will identify mastery of the identified priority skill.

SEL Competency Rubric

The SEL Competency Rubric is designed to help teachers identify what mastery looks like for the SEL competency (skills) they are teaching. Ultimately, we want students to independently demonstrate and generalize the taught skills; this is reflected as the highest point value in your rubric.

In the three blank columns of the form on the next page, teacher teams will insert mastery descriptors.

Note: This rubric is blank to allow each teacher to select developmentally appropriate mastery indicators reflective of their group of students and grade level/department. For example, social awareness looks different for a kindergartener at an elementary school than it does for an alternative education student or in a comprehensive high school. It is also important for the SEL Competency Rubric to be developed in a collaborative team. This will build both collective ownership of the finished product and clarity regarding what mastery will look like. We do not recommend that this document is created by one person and distributed to a faculty, because it will only be clear to the one who created it, which may result in a faculty feeling like there is "one more thing being thrown at them." Their voice *must* be part of the process.

Remember: Start with your highest priority from Phase 1. This is your entry point, not your final destination.

SEL Competency	Internalized Mastery Student independently demonstrates (2)	Emergent Mastery Student demonstrates with prompt or cue (1)	Minimal to No Mastery Student inconsistently demonstrates or does not demonstrate (0)
Relationship Skills			
Responsible Decision Making			
Social Awareness			
Self-Management			
Self-Awareness			

PHASE 3: SEL TEACHING PROCESS

Embed the priority SEL competency and related skill(s) into the SEL Teaching Process, which includes identify, teach, model, and reinforce.

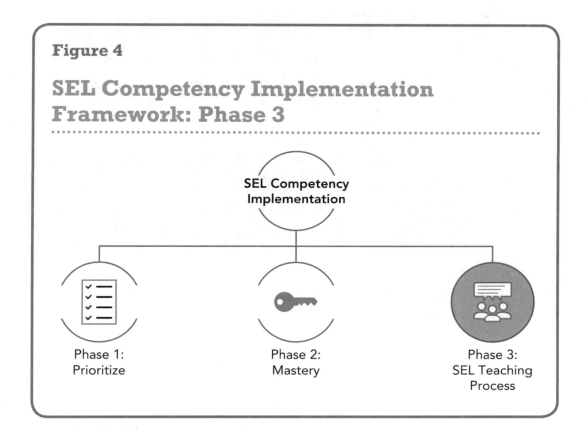

Figure 4

SEL Competency Implementation Framework: Phase 3

SEL Competency Implementation

Phase 1:
Prioritize

Phase 2:
Mastery

Phase 3:
SEL Teaching
Process

What Happens in the SEL Teaching Process Phase?

You will utilize the SEL Teaching Process embedded in the SEL From a Distance Planning Template provided in this section as a way to effectively plan and implement the tools and processes that match your identified SEL need focus areas.

What Is the SEL Teaching Process?

The SEL Teaching Process is a best-practice approach in teaching SEL competencies (skills) and includes the identify, teach, model, and reinforce stages.

Figure 5

The SEL Teaching Process

Identify
Based on schoolwide and/or classroom data, the leadership team or teacher team identifies common SEL competencies necessary for student success and develops problem of practice statements and success criteria.

Teach
Students are explicitly taught using a variety of modalities the focus SEL competency skill(s) schoolwide or in every learning environment (or both).

Model
The taught skills are demonstrated (modeled) by the educators on a daily basis by providing examples.

Reinforce
Taught skill is reinforced on an ongoing basis (daily, weekly, monthly, etc.).

Using the SEL Teaching Process and the SEL From a Distance Planning Template will help you learn how to implement SEL effectively with the tools and processes we provide in this book.

Note: In Chapter 8, there is a completed sample of an SEL From a Distance Planning Template as a reference.

The SEL From a Distance Planning Template on the next page is designed to help educators plan effective SEL instruction using the tools and processes provided. The template includes the core components of effective SEL Teaching Process—identify, teach, model, and reinforce—for each day of SEL instruction.

Definition of SEL Planning Template Terms

SEL Competency Focus is defined as one of the five SEL competencies: Relationship Skills, Responsible Decision Making, Social Awareness, Self-Management, and Self-Awareness.

SEL Competency Deconstructed Skill is defined as the deconstructed component of the selected focus SEL competency.

SEL From a Distance Planning Template

SEL Competency Focus:

SEL Competency Deconstructed Skill:

This week's mastery evidence (how will you know if your students have mastered the skill?):

Week of:

Monday	Tuesday	Wednesday	Thursday	Friday
Identify	Identify	Identify	Identify	Identify
Teach	Teach	Teach	Teach	Teach
Model	Model	Model	Model	Model
Reinforce	Reinforce	Reinforce	Reinforce	Reinforce

SEL Competency	SEL Competency Deconstructed Skill
Relationship Skills	Communication
	Social engagement
	Relationship building
	Teamwork
Responsible Decision Making	Identifying problems
	Analyzing situations
	Solving problems
	Evaluation
	Reflecting
	Ethical responsibility
Social Awareness	Perspective taking
	Empathy
	Appreciating diversity
	Respect for others
Self-Management	Impulse control
	Stress management
	Self-discipline
	Self-motivation
	Goal setting
	Organizational skills
Self-Awareness	Identifying emotions
	Accurate self-perception
	Recognizing strengths
	Self-confidence
	Self-efficacy

Images source: istock.com/-VICTOR-.

Before you move on to the tools and processes for each SEL competency, develop your common language. If you do not understand the *why* (purpose) of this work, the *what* and the *how* (common definition and alignment of the tools and processes) will not matter.

SEL Common Definition:		
Why SEL?	**What SEL?**	**How SEL?**

With any implementation comes its own set of challenges, and as we have all been made aware during the pandemic, we need to learn how to adapt to the needs of our students. One way to be proactive about challenges that lie ahead with implementation of this work is to learn about and watch out for the key contributing factors that impact implementation of any initiative, especially SEL implementation from a distance.

What Is the Systemic Behavior Gap? How Can We Avoid It?

Figure 6 is a visual representation of what we refer to as the Systemic Behavior Gap (adapted from Hannigan, Hannigan, Mattos, & Buffum, 2020), which we define as the gap between the implementation of behavior initiatives and the collective responsibility of all. The reason we want to point this out is because this gap already existed with in-person SEL implementation, so it will just widen from a distance if we are not intentional. In context with the SEL work from a distance, here are the pitfalls and guidelines for success:

Lack of communication: Transparent dialogue is necessary between you and your students, families, and other stakeholders.

Lack of collaboration: Working together is necessary with your students, families, and other stakeholders.

Lack of coordination: Resource alignment is necessary for yourself, your students, their families, and other stakeholders.

Lack of capacity building: Learning together is necessary for all.

Lack of collective ownership: We all (student, teacher, families, other stakeholders) take responsibility for the success of every student.

Figure 6

Systemic Behavior Gap

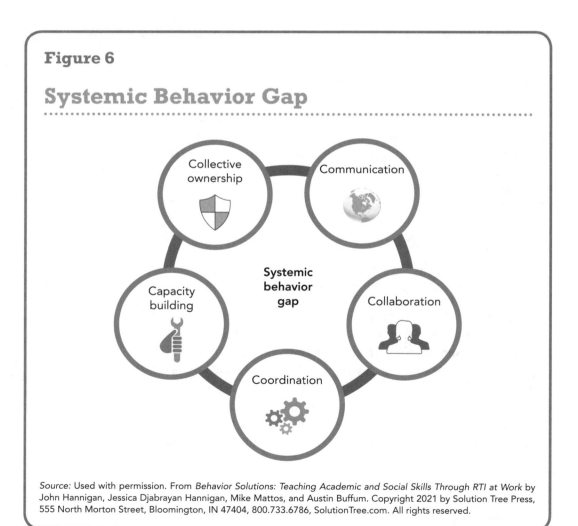

The point of sharing the Systemic Behavior Gap prior to beginning the next sections is to make sure you are mindful of the contributing factors that will impede implementation so they can be avoided. Any classroom, department, grade level, and schoolwide implementation failure can be traced back to any of these five contributing factors.

The Thinking Behind the Tools and Processes (Connecting SEL to Real Life)

In the next chapters of this book, you will be provided with a brief definition of each of the five SEL competencies, along with tools and processes for each. We want you to understand that these tools and processes can be adjusted to meet the needs of your classroom or student developmental levels. Our goal is to give you a starting point that will help you visualize how SEL can be implemented in a way that is an authentic, natural, and intentional part of your learning environment.

As you learned about the phases in the SEL Implementation Framework, we first asked you to take the priority rating scale as a method to prioritize and target the SEL area you find the most essential at this point in time; this in no way implies the rest is not important. The rating scale simply allows teacher teams and schools to identify the first step in their journey. We then walk you through how to decide mastery using a rubric designed to capture what evidence indicators are relevant to your needs. In addition, we provide you with an SEL teaching process and an SEL planning tool to ensure identify, teach, model, and reinforce components as part of the instruction to maximize impact.

As you read about the tools and process in each of the chapters, divided by the five SEL competencies, we provide steps for each process and a suggested application, but again, you decide what is best for your students and setting. These are all proven and tested and beneficial for all grade levels. Our purpose is to intentionally keep the implementation as straightforward and practical as possible whether in a distance, hybrid, or in-person environment. More important, we want you to understand the processes and gauge the impact of the work on your students.

How Best to Utilize
the Next Sections of This Book

As you read this section, process all the components of the indicators one at a time. Consider how you are going to proceed through these competencies and utilize the tools and processes provided. Also, make a time-bound commitment after starting each competency using the SEL Template Planning Guide to ensure that progress is being made. Remember, this will not all happen in one day; it is better to focus on each skill with full fidelity to ensure students are learning. Implementation is not just about the SEL tool, but rather the intentional process behind the tool to help your students master each skill. In addition, our tools can be utilized from a distance using features connected with your school's online platform and your basic Office or Google features by sharing your screen. We do not want to make this more complex than it needs to be. Furthermore, this book is written to provide ideas for whole-class, small-group, and individual instruction. We suggest these skills be taught to all students, but we recognize that some tools and processes could be removed for students who have mastered, or continued for the students who need additional teaching or reteaching opportunities for mastery.

Use the following organizational template to take notes on your progress through each core SEL competency and on the tools and processes connected to them. Also, note that some of the tools and processes can be converted across other competencies as well. We categorized them to be utilized by skill and a starting point.

SEL Competency	SEL Competency Deconstructed Skill	Tool	Process (steps)	Modality of Teaching (explicit instruction, wrong way right way, scenarios, project based, etc.)	Frequency (1× a week, 2× a week, monthly, quarterly, etc.)	Other Notes

PART II

THE TOOLS AND PROCESSES

SEL is not a thing to do. It is the way of being—all day every day—in any setting.

RELATIONSHIP SKILLS TOOLS AND PROCESSES

In this chapter, you will find the definition of the social and emotional learning (SEL) competency Relationships Skills, the deconstructed components necessary for mastering this SEL competency, and tools and processes for each. Although we have provided here some of our most effective SEL tools and processes, you can adjust, add to, and refine them with other tools. Remember, the goal is to go beyond just a tool to an intentional process that requires you to *identify, teach, model,* and *reinforce* the SEL skills students need for success in school and life.

SEL Competency: Relationship Skills

What are relationship skills? Relationship skills are the ability to establish and maintain healthy and rewarding relationships with diverse individuals and groups and to communicate clearly, listen well, cooperate with others, resist inappropriate social pressure, negotiate conflict constructively, and seek and offer help when needed (see casel.org).

Simply put, we want our students to have the skills they need to communicate effectively, problem solve peacefully, and have positive interactions with individuals and groups in multiple settings in school and life. This SEL competency is deconstructed to capture this meaning.

SEL competency deconstructed skills: Communication, social engagement, relationship building, teamwork

In this section, we have provided you with a tool and process for each of the deconstructed skills required for effective mastery of the SEL competency Relationship Skills.

Note: Although you are seeing distance learning examples of these tools and processes, this does not mean they cannot be converted to in-person or hybrid settings. The way to look at it is this: If you can do it from a distance, you can do it in person or in a hybrid setting as well.

Menu of Tools and Processes for the SEL Competency

RELATIONSHIP SKILLS

- ☐ Communication
- ☐ Social engagement
- ☐ Relationship building
- ☐ Teamwork

Communication

TOOL 1: CHOICE WORDS

Process: Operationally define Choice Words for your classroom with your students. Review the difference between words utilized at home/with friends and words utilized in the classroom or in a future work setting. Ask for and integrate student input/voice into your definition of Choice Words so there is a shared understanding and agreement of its meaning and what is expected.

Tip: Emphasize to your students that it is always important for them to feel comfortable being who they are, but it is also important they learn how to respect the language expected in different settings while staying true to themselves.

Post the Choice Words definition as a sign or reference for students entering the in-person or virtual classroom.

Remind the students of Choice Words daily as they are entering the classroom or as you start instruction.

Tip: Choice Words can be integrated into your classroom agreements or norms.

TOOL 2: EMPATHIC LISTENING

Process: Define empathic listening. Empathic listening can be defined as the intentional listening to hear what someone is telling you.

Share for 2 minutes while students listen (*silent* and *listen* have the same letters; remind the students to listen silently). Prompt students to take notes as you are speaking about a topic or experience.

When you are finished, students will talk to a partner or the whole class about what they heard using the sentence frame "I heard you say . . ." or "I heard you share. . . ."

In partners, one student shares with the other student. A topic or experience can be provided ahead of time, or it can be a topic the class has decided on together. The partner practices listening and repeats back using the same sentence frame: "I heard you say . . ." or "I heard you share. . . ." Students can be organized in groups of two in breakout rooms.

Reflect on the experience: What was it like to talk to someone, and what was it like to listen to someone?

TOOL 3: "AIR SHARE" TIME

Process: Give a prompt (e.g., "What is something that is challenging to you with distance learning? Reflect on the biggest challenge for you during distance learning. Reflect on your biggest personal achievements.")

Students have 3 minutes to think about the prompt while music is playing in the background (post the prompt in a slide or on a shared document).

After the 3 minutes, each student gets an opportunity for a 20-second "Air Share" Time to respond and summarize their response in 10 words or less (e.g., "Distance learning has helped me understand the importance of relationships.").

· ·

TOOL 4: APPOINTMENT CLOCK

Process: Give students a prompt to think about for 2 minutes. After 2 minutes, move students into group appointment chat rooms.

In the chat room, each student has 1 minute of uninterrupted time to respond to a prompt (e.g., Share something you are excited about with distance learning. Share a distance learning "win.").

As each student is sharing for 1 minute, the other students are taking notes (a template to ask questions is provided below).

After each student has shared in the group, provide 10 minutes of question-and-answer time. Request that each student ask at least one question.

What follows is the template to help keep students on track during this small-group exercise:

Two-minute topic: _____		
Student-Sharing Name	**Questions I Have**	**Responses**

TOOL 5: PROPER TEXT ETIQUETTE (WRONG WAY, RIGHT WAY)

Process: Teach wrong/right way communication in a virtual setting using the examples provided below. Show students the wrong and right way of interpreting and using text in communication in a virtual setting (e.g., ALL CAPS, **bold**, *italics*, sarcasm/jokes) and explain how these can be misinterpreted in a digital space.

Proper Text Etiquette

There are times caps help to put emphasis on a word or phrase, but more often than not, your audience feels like you're YELLING AT THEM!

Bold, *italicized*, <u>underlined</u>, and "quotation marks" in text can come across as aggressive, sarcastic, or rude.

Examples:

- Teacher interaction: After all, this assignment was "optional" back in February.

- That's not what *you* said.

- Could you please **reply ASAP**?!!

- Student interaction with another student in a debate: **I DO NOT AGREE! THAT IS STUPID! IDK.**

How to Email Your Teacher

- Topic: Two-to-five word summary of the email, like "Assignment help."
- Greet the teacher and tell them why you are writing the email. "Good afternoon, I am writing because I am feeling overwhelmed with some of the assignments."
- Wrap up by saying "thank you" and signing your name.

Have students come up with other ways text can be misinterpreted and develop a wrong way, right way with a partner(s) for their selected example. You can do this as a joint slide deck so each student or partner group can add to it and present.

Slide Template

- Insert your names.
- Insert one way text can be misinterpreted in a virtual setting.
- Wrong way
- Right way

Social Engagement

TOOL 1: STUDENT SELF-CHECK SURVEY

Process: Poll or survey your students using the following prompts. Use the information from the class to share findings with the students. Get their feedback on improvements to help all students feel safe to engage.

Student Check Survey

Please respond (True/False). The goal is to get to where you feel as though you can circle True for all the items:

• I feel safe to participate in class	**T or F**
• I feel like I can advocate for my needs in class	**T or F**
• I feel like my classmates will support me if needed	**T or F**
• I feel like I have a voice	**T or F**
• I feel like my teacher will help me if I need it	**T or F**
• I feel like I can express myself	**T or F**

TOOL 2: CLASSROOM MANTRAS

Process: Select your classroom mantras and reinforce them daily.

Examples of how you can share your mantras from a distance include the following:

- Embed them into the class warm-up.
- Play a slideshow with the mantras at the beginning of instruction.
- Make the mantras your wallpaper or background.
- Include them in every email or communication; post them in your virtual classroom.

Classroom Mantra Examples

• You are loved.	• You are valued.
• You are welcome.	• You are heard.
• You belong.	• You are seen.
• You are beautiful.	• You are safe.
• You are worthy.	• You are appreciated for your differences.
• You have a voice.	

TOOL 3: SERVICE LEARNING PROJECTS

Process: Select classroom service learning projects. Try to do this at least monthly. Describe the purpose of the project to the students and give them choices on what project they want to participate in as a class to give back to the community. When the project is completed, have students reflect on the project and how it helped them engage with their classmates and the community.

Examples of service learning projects include the following:

- Write letters of encouragement to individuals in a nursing home or others in need.
- Write letters or make videos for hospital staff thanking them for their service.
- Identify frontline responders and research how their jobs have been impacted. Develop a plan for what they need and how we can support them.
- Interview adults and other students, asking them how they are doing during this time (e.g., how COVID-19 has impacted their lives, businesses).
- Develop a student guide to thriving during crisis individually, in groups, or as a class.
- Create an online "stay positive" campaign/hashtag with a focused purpose and plan with goals.
- Create get well cards or posters and share with anyone in need.
- Research an area in the community that needs attention and develop a timeline and proposed actions for the community to address the need (e.g., hot spots, access to technology).
- Read a book or watch a movie that describes a pandemic and write about the key similarities and differences based on your real-life experiences.
- Write letters or poems or create a story. Record yourself reading the letter, poem, or story.
- Create a YouTube video or podcast for students sharing ways you can help one another.

Relationship Building

TOOL 1: "GETTING TO KNOW ME" EXERCISE

Process:

- **Step 1:** Create a joint classroom PowerPoint or slides in whatever modality you prefer.

- **Step 2:** Create a sample of a "getting to know me" slide of yourself and describe the essential components. Students can use words, videos (link to short video), images, drawings, and so on to answer each prompt.

Your name	Love to do for fun	Your strongest trait	Best teacher from personal experience, film, TV, etc. (*Why?*)
Learning style preference	Learning style nonpreference	Future goals	Helps when I am upset or overwhelmed

- **Step 3:** Have students create their slide.

- **Step 4:** Share out in whatever modality you prefer, one-on-one with you, small groups, whole class. Make sure to designate time for each student to share.

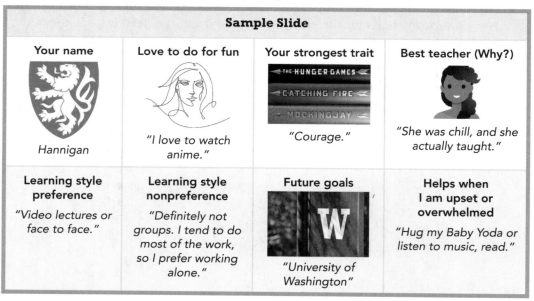

Sample Slide

Your name	Love to do for fun	Your strongest trait	Best teacher (Why?)
Hannigan	"I love to watch anime."	"Courage."	"She was chill, and she actually taught."
Learning style preference "Video lectures or face to face."	**Learning style nonpreference** "Definitely not groups. I tend to do most of the work, so I prefer working alone."	**Future goals** "University of Washington"	**Helps when I am upset or overwhelmed** "Hug my Baby Yoda or listen to music, read."

Image sources: istock.com/gregobagel, istock.com/apatpoh, istock.com/grafico2013, istock.com/shaunl, istock.com/Genestro.

TOOL 2: "GETTING TO KNOW EACH OTHER" BINGO

Process: Have students submit some facts about themselves (What is my favorite food, favorite song, favorite slogan, something people don't really know about me, etc.) in an online survey (e.g., Google form).

Complete the BINGO card and see if the students can guess who by raising their virtual hand or by using the chat feature. Stamp the BINGO card using the annotation feature on Zoom, or by copying and pasting a stamp image. Use the BINGO card once a week with the class.

"Getting to Know Each Other" BINGO			
Loves to fish	Has been in a movie	Was born in Lebanon	Loves to eat breakfast foods all the time ☆
Loves *Star Wars*	Has 10 animals	Loves to draw	Loves to write songs ☆
Wants to be an engineer	Loves to cook	Has a best friend in another town	Loves 1980s movies ☆
Plays video games when stressed	Loves to try new foods	Can speak three languages	Is an only child ☆

Teamwork

TOOL 1: ROLES/RESPONSIBILITIES (JOBS)

Process: Establish a roles/responsibilities protocol. Teach students the roles and responsibilities of all the jobs in the virtual classroom environment. Have students put the roles and responsibilities in their own words. Also, teach students how to select roles quickly when put into a small group.

Identify the roles/responsibilities for your students during whole-class and small-group exercises. Provide a virtual prompt to remind them of their roles/responsibilities prior to sending them into small groups.

Role	Responsibility (Job Description)
Classroom greeter	Greets anyone who virtually enters the classroom
Student class co-host	Helps teacher as a co-host
Recorder	Takes notes in small-group activities
Reporter	Shares out in small-group activities
Facilitator job leader	Leads the discussion or task given to the group, makes sure each person gets a chance to contribute
Timekeeper	Keeps time and gives 5-minute and 1-minute warnings
Active participant	Participates in the discussion even without a specific role

Note: For younger students, you can use visuals to explain roles/responsibilities.

TOOL 2: CLASSROOM CHALLENGES

Process: Select or establish a classroom challenge (assign a timeline to the challenge and develop a goal as a class). Remind students of the classroom challenge daily and provide updates on goal attainment. Have students come up with ways to promote the challenge through social media (hashtags, videos, etc.).

Note: Challenges can be set up for 2-month periods or as long as needed. Each challenge needs a goal at the beginning that is messaged out and taught to the student body (needs to be measurable). Updates on progress on goals need to be reported to the student body. Rewards for meeting the challenges should be set up accordingly.

Sample Challenges				
Type of Challenge	**Goal of Challenge**	**Reward of Meeting the Challenge**	**Messaging Out and Teaching Challenge**	**Dates of Challenge (months or all year)**
Virtual Classroom Agreement Challenge	Decrease in number of minor and major virtual classroom disruptions by 50% compared to previous month	Free Dress Days (theme dress days)	Announcements, Classroom Instruction	September–October
Upstander Challenge #ittakes1 to stand up, report, ask for help for someone who needs it	Decrease student self-reports of being bullied 50% compared to baseline survey	Virtual Class Dance (student can DJ)	Announcements, Classroom Instruction	November–December
Attendance Challenge	Improve attendance by 50%	Lunch time virtual privileges/activities	Announcements, Classroom Instruction	January–February
Being Mindful Challenge	All students participating in daily mindful minutes exercises	Free choice	Announcements, Classroom Instruction	March–April
Gratitude Challenge	All students participating in daily gratitude statement exercises	Homework pass	Announcements, Classroom Instruction	May–June

TOOL 3: WEEKLY TEACHING FOCUS AREA AND REINFORCEMENT SCHEDULE

Process: Focus on one skill at a time each week, and have intentional reinforcement of the demonstrated skills.

Week 1 Reinforce Daily	Week 2 Reinforce Daily	Week 3 Reinforce Daily	Week 4 Reinforce Daily
Self-control Daily point expectation (20 points a day). Assign points for students demonstrating self-control.	**On-task** Daily point expectation (20 points a day). Assign points for students demonstrating on-task behaviors.	**Achievement** Daily point expectation (20 points a day). Assign points for students demonstrating achievement.	**Respect** Daily point expectation (20 points a day). Assign points for students demonstrating respect.

Self-Control Weekly Challenge	Weekly Challenge Winner Categories	Sample Virtual Prizes
Highest self-control classroom points (e.g., points are given daily for students demonstrating behaviors identified on the classroom agreement related to self-control)	Highest-classroom-point winner Department winner Grade-level winner Student per grade-level winner Teacher winner for assigning most points Overall student winner	Homework pass VIP student of the day VIP staff of the day VIP department or grade level of the day Student-choice class activity Student spotlight on social media or during class Student becomes partner teacher of the day Virtual badge for character Virtual lunch time with teacher Play song or favorite appropriate clips for class Student-determined incentive Skip a meeting pass Administrator teaches your class for the day Classroom special online visitor Free-time choice for class Extended virtual break

TOOL 4: CLASSROOM OR INDIVIDUAL REWARDS CHART

Process: At the beginning of the week, solicit student feedback on something they would like to earn as a class. Awards could include free-choice time, playing music, virtual classroom dance party, or drawing time. Move a star to the box for each day of demonstrating the appropriate skill. For example, if this was a participation weekly goal, there could be a set goal the class has to meet to earn the star for the day. You can do this with individual students as well and have them select the goal with you. This template can be inserted into a slide deck and quickly pulled up with a shared screen to discuss with the class or individually in a breakout room.

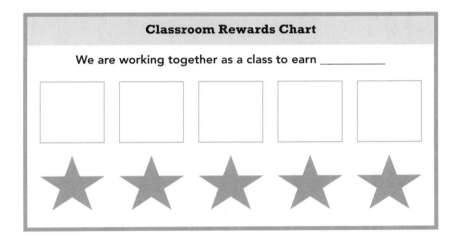

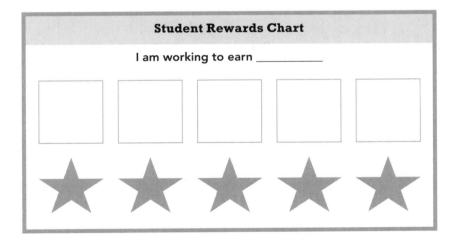

You have reached the end of the Relationship SEL competency chapter. Now may be a good time to pause and see if you can capture some of the tools and processes aligned with the priority SEL competency you identified at the beginning of this book. In addition, if you need a reference, see a completed template in Chapter 8 on page 122.

SEL From a Distance Planning Template

SEL Competency Focus:

SEL Competency Deconstructed Skill:

This week's mastery evidence (how will you know if your students have mastered the skill?):

Week of:

Monday	Tuesday	Wednesday	Thursday	Friday
Identify	Identify	Identify	Identify	Identify
Teach	Teach	Teach	Teach	Teach
Model	Model	Model	Model	Model
Reinforce	Reinforce	Reinforce	Reinforce	Reinforce

RESPONSIBLE DECISION MAKING TOOLS AND PROCESSES

In this chapter, you will find the social and emotional learning (SEL) competency definition of Responsible Decision Making, the deconstructed components necessary for mastering it, and tools and processes for each. Although we have provided you with some of our most effective SEL tools and processes, you can adjust, add to, and refine them with other tools. Remember, the goal is to go beyond just a tool to an intentional process that requires you to *identify, teach, model,* and *reinforce* the SEL skills students need for success in school and in life.

SEL Competency: Responsible Decision Making

What is responsible decision making? It is the ability to make constructive choices about personal behavior and social interactions based on ethical standards, safety concerns, and social norms; to realistically evaluate the consequences of various actions; and to consider the well-being of oneself and others (see casel.org).

Simply put, we want our students to have the skills they need to know the difference between right and wrong, make thought-through decisions that impact themselves and the community, problem solve, and take accountability by acknowledging and learning from mistakes. This SEL competency is deconstructed to capture these goals by the following skills:

SEL competency deconstructed skills: Identifying problems, analyzing situations, solving problems, evaluating, reflecting, ethical responsibility

In this section, we have provided you with a tool and process for each of the deconstructed skills required for effective mastery of the SEL competency Responsible Decision Making.

Note: Although you are seeing distance learning examples of these tools and processes, this does not mean they cannot be converted to in-person or hybrid settings. The way to look at it is this: If you can do it from a distance, you can do it in person, or in a hybrid setting as well.

Menu of Tools and Processes for the SEL Competency

RESPONSIBLE DECISION MAKING

- ☐ Identifying problems
- ☐ Analyzing situations
- ☐ Solving problems
- ☐ Evaluating
- ☐ Reflecting
- ☐ Ethical responsibility

Identifying Problems

TOOL 1: VIRTUAL LEARNING PROMPTS

Process: Provide a prompt to your students daily or weekly. Have them discuss in groups using the questions below with the prompts as a guide. Students can also write about the prompts or create a video or image to help demonstrate their responses. Have the students come up with their own prompts related to the focus area.

Sample Prompts

Self-Control Prompt: The teacher is teaching a lesson to the class online. Mark notices the chat feature is open for private chatting (teacher forgot to turn it off). He continues to distract other students during the lesson by sending them private inappropriate chat messages the teacher cannot see. What can Mark do to demonstrate self-control in the virtual learning environment?

> **Identify the problem.**
>
> Why is this a problem?
>
> What can the student do instead?

On-Task Prompt: Michelle is bored during an online group assignment. She decides to shut off her camera and press mute. She begins to watch TikTok videos on her phone until the group online discussion part of the instruction is over. What can Michelle do to demonstrate on-task behaviors in the virtual learning environment?

> **Identify the problem.**
>
> Why is this a problem?
>
> What can the student do instead?

Achievement Prompt: Angel's teacher assigns reading prior to logging in for the class discussion and assignment. Angel decides that he will not read ahead of time and that he will be fine filling in the responses by text messaging his friends for the answers during class. What can Angel do to demonstrate achievement behaviors in the virtual learning environment?

> **Identify the problem.**
>
> Why is this a problem?
>
> What can the student do instead?

Respect Prompt: Janice disagrees with another classmate during an online debate on a topic about which she cares deeply. Instead of responding to this classmate with civility, she begins to interrupt and use features (bold/CAPS) demonstrating she is yelling. What can Janice do to demonstrate respect behaviors in the virtual learning environment?

> **Identify the problem.**
>
> Why is this a problem?
>
> What can the student do instead?

TOOL 2: STUDENT SURVEY

Process: Students are asked to share their input (voice) in identifying the areas of need in the virtual classroom setting in alignment with the pre-existing classroom or school expectations.

Students are given the survey aligned with the classroom expectations to provide feedback in a virtual setting.

The information is shared with the students, and solutions are discussed as a class.

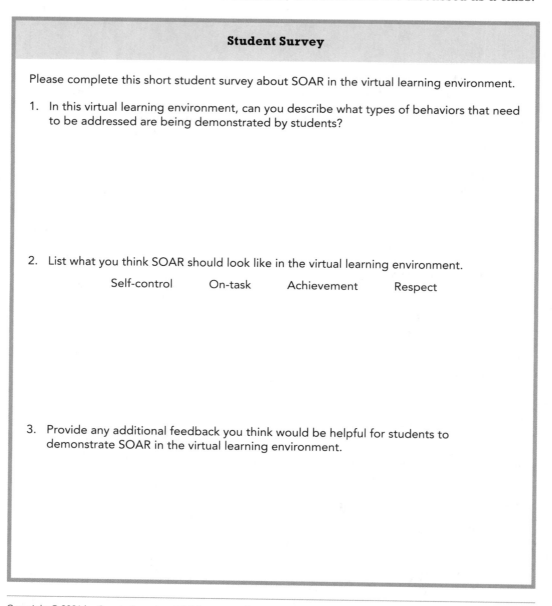

Student Survey

Please complete this short student survey about SOAR in the virtual learning environment.

1. In this virtual learning environment, can you describe what types of behaviors that need to be addressed are being demonstrated by students?

2. List what you think SOAR should look like in the virtual learning environment.

    Self-control   On-task   Achievement   Respect

3. Provide any additional feedback you think would be helpful for students to demonstrate SOAR in the virtual learning environment.

Analyzing Situations

TOOL 1: PROJECT ASSIGNMENT TEMPLATE

Process: Post a situation impacting your classroom as a collective (e.g., misuse of online features). In small groups, have students analyze the problem with multiple data points using this project assignment template as a prompt. Have each group share out their findings.

Project Assignment Template

What is the problem behavior (e.g., misuse of online tool features)?

Why do you think based on your collected data (stakeholder interviews and/or research) this behavior is occurring in our class (e.g., attention seeking, lack of social skills, students bored)?

1. Research ways to help students use online features appropriately. What are some ways to prevent misuse of these features? What have you learned from this assignment?

2. Develop a project to create proper use of online features prevention awareness. The project needs to include the following: definition and examples of how students misuse online features (e.g., chat rooms), ways to prevent misuse, and lessons learned.

3. Share the project or newly developed tool to selected stakeholders.

TOOL 1: HOW TO HAVE VIRTUAL CLASSROOM MEETINGS IN 20 MINUTES OR LESS

Process:

- **Step 1: Preparation (4 minutes):** Teach all students the purpose and roles of a virtual classroom meeting. The purpose is to have a safe space to discuss difficult topics and feelings and/or problem solve specific issues/questions/ challenges taking place in the classroom, school, or community. *Tips:* Have a process where students can also submit questions or topics anonymously for consideration. Set up a consistent schedule for classroom meetings (e.g., every Monday, twice a week), but also allow for impromptu meetings as needed. Here are some sample topics or questions:

  o How can we improve student engagement during this time?

  o How are you being impacted by physical distancing, loss of social connections, virtual learning, etc.?

  o Share some strategies that have helped you move forward during this crisis.

  o What has been the most challenging thing for you during this crisis?

- **Step 2: Whole-Group Virtual Meeting (4 minutes):** Post the topic or question, explain context, and allow for students to process on their own by jotting down their own thoughts for a minute. Remind them of the importance of their voice in the breakout rooms. Review roles, remind them of virtual classroom agreements, and assign them to their breakout rooms (five to six per group).

- **Step 3: Small-Group Virtual Meeting (6 minutes):** If you want to preset the groups, you can have the students rename themselves with their group number. In the small group, students identify roles. The virtual classroom leader in the group will facilitate this process. Each person has 30 seconds to respond to the prompt. Recorder will take notes. Reporter will share out a few items.

- **Step 4: Closing and Commitments (6 minutes):** Repose the prompt or question. Allow time for share out from each group. Synthesize what you heard and type up a classroom closing or commitment for the meeting (keep an ongoing log). Each student also privately writes down their commitment. Meeting closes. If actions are decided, they should be put in place based on the meeting feedback.

Classroom Meeting Log			
Classroom Meeting Topic/Date	Focus SEL Competency	Classroom Meeting Share Out Ideas	Classroom Meeting Commitments

TOOL 2: RESTORATIVE AGREEMENT FORM

Process: Introduce the critical steps for coming to a restorative agreement when there is a conflict:

Steps
1. Acknowledging injustice or hurt
2. Hearing each side of the story
3. Taking actions necessary to restore
4. Coming to an agreement

Teachers can provide a scenario in which two students had a conflict and walk them through how to utilize the process or form on the next page. Students can work with a partner to discuss a conflict they have had in the past and what steps they took or did not take. Students can share out.

Note: Teachers can also use this with small groups of students with actual conflict that is brought to them for resolution. Students can also help conduct a respect agreement with other students.

Restorative Agreement Form

Date of Meeting: _____

Disputants

_____   _____   _____

_____   _____   _____

Referral Source

Administrator   Teacher   Student   Self   Other _____

Conflict Information

What is the conflict about?

_____

_____

_____

1. Did we recognize an injustice/violation? YES   NO   Other _____

2. Did we restore equity? Apology for injustices/violations

        Nothing necessary beyond this meeting   Other _____

3. Future Intentions (AGREEMENT/CONTRACT)

We agreed to prevent the problem from happening again by:

_____

_____

_____

Student Signatures: _____   _____

Student Signatures: _____   _____

4. Follow-Up Meeting

We agreed to meet again for a follow-up meeting. Follow-up meeting date: _____

Student Signatures: _____   _____

Student Signatures: _____   _____

Follow-Up Results

_____

_____

_____

Evaluating

TOOL 1: WRITE "YOUR NEW STORY" PROMPT

Process: Talk to the students about learning from their mistakes and self-evaluating their actions. Let them know part of self-evaluation requires them to acknowledge a poor choice they have made. Have them think of a scenario when they made a mistake, and have them individually complete this form first. Ask students to address an envelope and send or email it to themselves. Remind the students they have an opportunity to rewrite their story each day.

Write "Your New Story" Prompt

Name: _____ Date: _____

Who am I?

What are some poor choices I have made in the past at school (my old story)?

What do I want to see for myself (my new story) when it comes to behavior and academics in school?

How do I plan on making this new story come true?

What help do I need to make this new story come true?

Student signature of commitment to My New Story:

_____

Reflecting

TOOL 1: THINK SHEETS

Process: With the whole class, small groups, or individual students, teach students how to reflect by using these questions as a guide. Have students individually complete the Think Sheet first, and then walk them through each prompt. You can also have students use the Think Sheets to practice with each other.

Think Sheet
What did you do?
Why was that behavior inappropriate?
Who did you hurt?

(Continued)

(Continued)

What were you trying to accomplish?

Next time you have that goal, how will you meet it without hurting anybody?

How will you ask for help?

Think Sheet for Younger Students

I was feeling...

SAD SILLY MAD EMBARRASSED AFRAID/WORRIED BOSSY

I wanted...

____ attention ____ to have fun ____ to get my own way ____ to be left alone

____ someone to listen to me ____ I was already mad ____ other _____

I hurt _____'s ____ body ____ feelings

____ friendships/reputation ____ property when I _____

_____

_____

I could have _____

_____

_____

Student Signature _____

Parent Signature _____ **Date** _____

Images source: istock.com/ctermit.

Tip: DocuSign or other electronic signature methods can be utilized for this form.

TOOL 2: APOLOGY TEMPLATE COMPONENTS

Process: Talk to students about the difference between a generic and an authentic apology. Have students think of someone they have or have wanted to apologize to. Have them use this template to complete a letter. Reflect as a class.

Apology Letter Template Components

Write an apology letter that includes the following components:

- Address the person you have impacted due to your behavior.
- Identify and own the behavior that put you in this position.
- Acknowledge the hurt you may have caused due to your behavior.
- Identify the function of your behavior.
- Express your apology to the person.
- Provide three examples of what you have learned from this experience.
- Provide three examples demonstrating what will prevent you from engaging in this type of behavior again.
- Assure the person that this will never happen again.
- Sign the letter as a contract to your apology.

TOOL 3: VIRTUAL JOURNAL WRITING

Process: Provide a topic and time for students to write or draw in their virtual journal about. You can set up a Google sheet for each student, so only you and the student have access to the journal. The format of each page is as follows: Students will have 10 minutes to write. (A really good way to get a list of topics meaningful for students is to ask them.) Let them know that journaling is a strategy to help them work through some thoughts and emotions. Have students share out if they are comfortable. Ultimately, you want to create a culture where students feel safe and comfortable sharing their thoughts with their peers.

Virtual Journal Writing Template

Date: _____

Topic:

- About you (your perspective)
- Insecurities or concerns
- Questions you may have
- Suggestions and next steps

Ethical Responsibility

TOOL 1: UPSTANDER BEHAVIOR REHEARSAL CARDS

Process:

- **Step 1:** Ask students to check in. They should rate how well they met their behavior goals for the week (or another determined amount of time) between 1 and 5, and explain their self-rating.

    1 = I need to continue working on skills.

    2 = I am making improvements but need to continue working on skills.

    3 = I need to continue working on consistently using my learned skills.

    4 = I almost met all my goals for the week, with a few minor hiccups.

    5 = I met all my goals for the week.

- **Step 2:** Identify and define the focus behaviors and skills that the students will need to learn to demonstrate mastery.

- **Step 3:** Explain to the students the key behavior skills necessary to demonstrate mastery. Ask them to define the skills in their own words by writing or drawing them. Tell the students that they can look up the skills if they are unable to identify and define them.

- **Step 4:** As a small group or whole class, practice one of the behavior skill scenarios on the behavior rehearsal cards together by role playing. This helps students process the meaning of the behavior and practice the wrong way and right way to respond to the given scenario.

- **Step 5:** Put students in pairs or trios and ask them to practice the next skill together. Then, ask every student to come up with an example related to that card.

    o Ask students to write a journal entry in which they reflect and commit to how they will practice the newly learned skill or skills throughout the week (provide sentence strips if necessary—have the students initial them).

    o For the culmination, you can give the students behavior rehearsal cards as a mastery exam at the end of the week or when you are finished teaching them. You can ask them to provide written or oral responses based on each scenario or to do a culminating project related to their newly learned behaviors and skills, such as filming a video, solving a real-life problem, or completing a service learning project.

    o Repeat the process until the students have mastered all the skills.

Upstander Behavior Rehearsal Lesson Cards

WHY: To provide reteaching opportunities for students on upstander skills.

WHAT: Upstander Skills Behavior Rehearsal Lesson Cards (role-playing and practice opportunities)

HOW: Insert each card on a PowerPoint slide so students can see. Provide them with a copy of the PowerPoint to reference as you are also presenting it on your screen.

Additional Suggestions: Practice card or cards after completing Upstander Skills goal progress self-monitoring sheet first. Have students complete a journal entry in Upstander Skills journal explaining what they practiced, with the date and their commitment to practice. Assign homework to practice the skills on the card or cards and share how they practiced at the next session.

Aware	Supportive
You see a person getting teased by a group of students, but you don't say anything because no one else seems to mind.	You witness someone being picked on about something that happened over the weekend. No one except for the teacher is acknowledging this person because of the incident over the weekend.
What is the right way? *What is the wrong way?*	*What is the right way?* *What is the wrong way?*

Action Oriented	Speaks Up
You know there is a way to anonymously report bullying at your school, but you decide someone else should do it, not you.	You are close friends with the person who is bullying a younger student, but you do not tell him to stop. You laugh at his comments because you do not want him to stop being your friend.
What is the right way? *What is the wrong way?*	*What is the right way?* *What is the wrong way?*

Stands Up	Courageous
You know the bullying behavior you are seeing from some students toward others is not okay, but you do not want to say anything so you are not the next victim. *What is the right way?* *What is the wrong way?*	You decide to stay quiet about a bullying situation you have witnessed between a group of girls toward another girl over a boy. You want to say something, but you are afraid, so you don't. *What is the right way?* *What is the wrong way?*
Digital Citizen	**Leader**
You know of two or three students who are constantly the target of every online joke. Instead of stopping the behavior, you comment and like the mean posts online. *What is the right way?* *What is the wrong way?*	You are asked to get involved in a discussion about bullying behaviors at the school. You choose to not be honest about the bullying behaviors you have witnessed. *What is the right way?* *What is the wrong way?*
Inclusive	**Resourceful**
You notice the new student at the school is always left out and has no one to speak to or hang out with during break times. You feel bad but you do not want to risk missing anything going on with your group, so you continue as usual without inviting her to join. *What is the right way?* *What is the wrong way?*	You do not know how to get help for students who are being bullied and make no effort to find out. You figure someone else will do it and it is not your business. *What is the right way?* *What is the wrong way?*

You have reached the end of the Responsible Decision Making SEL competency chapter. Now may be a good time to pause and see if you can capture some of the tools and processes aligned with the priority SEL competency you identified at the beginning of this book. In addition, if you need a reference, see a completed template in Chapter 8 on page 122.

SEL From a Distance Planning Template				
SEL Competency Focus:				
SEL Competency Deconstructed Skill:				
This week's mastery evidence (how will you know if your students have mastered the skill?):				
Week of:				
Monday	**Tuesday**	**Wednesday**	**Thursday**	**Friday**
Identify	Identify	Identify	Identify	Identify
Teach	Teach	Teach	Teach	Teach
Model	Model	Model	Model	Model
Reinforce	Reinforce	Reinforce	Reinforce	Reinforce

SOCIAL AWARENESS TOOLS AND PROCESSES

In this chapter, you will find the social and emotional learning (SEL) competency definition of Social Awareness, the deconstructed components necessary for mastering this competency, and tools and processes for each. Although we have provided here some of our most effective SEL tools and processes, you can adjust, add to, or refine them with other tools. Remember, the goal is to go beyond just a tool to an intentional SEL process that requires you to *identify*, *teach*, *model*, and *reinforce* the SEL skills students need for success in school and in life.

SEL Competency: Social Awareness

What is social awareness? It is the ability to take the perspective of and empathize with others, including those from diverse backgrounds and cultures. Social Awareness includes the ability to understand social and ethical norms for behavior and to recognize family, school, and community resources and supports (see casel.org).

Simply put, we want our students to learn how to accept diverse perspectives, utilize resources, and become civil and empathic members of the community. This SEL competency is deconstructed to capture these goals by the following skills:

SEL competency deconstructed skills: Perspective taking, empathy, appreciating diversity, respect for others

In this section, we have provided you with a tool and process for each of the deconstructed skills required for effective mastery of the SEL competency Social Awareness.

Note: Although you are seeing distance learning examples of these tools and processes, this does not mean they cannot be converted to in-person or hybrid settings. The way to look at it is this: If you can do it from a distance, you can do it in person or in a hybrid setting as well.

Menu of Tools and Processes for the SEL Competency

SOCIAL AWARENESS

- ☐ Perspective taking
- ☐ Empathy
- ☐ Appreciating diversity
- ☐ Respect for others

Perspective Taking

TOOL 1: INTERVIEW TEMPLATE

Process: Talk to students about the importance of interviewing individuals to understand their perspectives. Talk to them about the four main components of a perspective-taking interview process: (1) acknowledging your perspective prior to the interview, (2) stakeholder voice (perceptions and feelings), (3) recapping what you heard with "I heard you say" statements, and (4) reflecting on your original perspective based on stakeholder input.

Interview Template

Assignment: Interview someone connected with your school (e.g., teacher, substitute, custodian, volunteer, other staff) and write a reflection addressing the questions using evidence from the interview template on the following page. Provide a copy of the reflection to the teacher and the individual interviewed. This project can be completed individually or in a small group.

Identify a topic or situation you will be interviewing about (e.g., poor behavior choice with a substitute teacher).

Prior to the interview please complete this section: What is your perspective around this topic or situation?

The example below is an interview with a substitute teacher in a virtual environment.

Stakeholder Voice (Perceptions and Feelings)

In your own words, can you share a little bit about your experience being a substitute teacher in a virtual classroom environment?

Why did you get into substitute teaching?

What are some challenges of being a substitute teacher in a virtual setting?

What are some opportunities related to being a substitute teacher in a virtual setting?

How should students behave when they have a substitute teacher?

Have you experienced disrespectful students while substitute teaching in a virtual setting?

How do you feel when students are not following classroom rules when you are substitute teaching?

Have you had positive experiences substitute teaching in a virtual environment?

What would be your ideal virtual classroom to substitute teach for?

Develop three additional questions to ask the substitute teacher:

1. _____
2. _____
3. _____

"I heard you say" statements:

I heard the *interviewee* say _____

I heard the *interviewee* say _____

I heard the *interviewee* say _____

Write your reflection here:

What did you learn about the *interviewee*'s perspective? How was this different from your initial perceptions of the situation? How was it the same?

TOOL 2: CYBERBULLYING PERSPECTIVE-TAKING SCENARIOS

Process: Share scenarios with students. Have them individually reflect first for 1–2 minutes. Split them up into groups to discuss their thoughts for 3–4 minutes, then recreate the groups so they discuss with another group. Share with the whole class and answer the questions together.

Scenario 1: You are at a party where other students are pressuring you to post a picture on social media that would embarrass another student. You feel pressured to fit in with the students.

- What would you do if you were in this situation to prevent cyberbullying?
- How do you think the other student would feel if you engaged in this behavior?
- Wrong way?
- Right way?
- What skill is necessary for someone to engage in the right way?

Scenario 2: Some of your schoolmates are creating fake online accounts so they can post mean comments on other students' accounts without anyone knowing who they are. They ask you to participate.

- What would you do if you were in this situation to prevent cyberbullying?
- How do you think the other students would feel if you engaged in this behavior?
- Wrong way?
- Right way?
- What skill is necessary for someone to engage in the right way?

Scenario 3: A student is dating someone you like. You feel angry at this person and think about making up a rumor and sharing it through as many online outlets as possible. Your friends are encouraging you to do so.

- What would you do if you were in this situation to prevent cyberbullying?
- How do you think the other student would feel if you engaged in this behavior?
- Wrong way?
- Right way?
- What skill is necessary for someone to engage in the right way?

TOOL 3: COMMUNITY SERVICE

Process: Community service refers to service that a person performs for the benefit of their local community.

Talk to students about the meaning of community service and the various ways students can give back (also in a virtual form). Post or email the students the community service cheat sheet and log to reference as you are talking. Gather some additional examples for each category with student input. Have students complete logs weekly. The signatures can be electronically gathered from whichever stakeholder you decide you want a weekly signature from. Weekly reflections about community service experience can also take place as a whole class or in small groups. You can even have a community service highlight from a few students each week explaining the activities they engaged in and why.

Community service opportunities can help students do the following:

- Step outside of their familiar environments and expand their horizons
- Strengthen their senses of civic engagement
- Broaden their educational, developmental, and social goals
- Bridge the generation gap by helping older (or younger) people
- Learn about the joys and challenges of volunteerism
- Find out that people are different and that it's okay!
- Learn how community decisions are made
- Practice new skills
- Gain confidence and feeling of self-worth
- Develop healthy attitudes toward physical fitness and much more

Different Types of Community Service Opportunities	
Community Service	**Social Experience**
<ul><li>Regular assistance to a person or community group</li><li>Clean up the local park</li><li>Recommended 1 hour per week</li></ul>	<ul><li>Take part in a community commemoration</li><li>Attend a community meeting</li><li>Find out about someone else's religious beliefs</li><li>Experience another culture</li><li>Recommended 1 hour per week</li></ul>
Physical Recreation	**Skills**
<ul><li>Develop a physical skill or learn a new one</li><li>Plant trees, flowers, or other plants</li><li>Help an elderly neighbor with the lawn</li><li>Recommended 1 hour per week</li></ul>	<ul><li>Develop a known skill or learn a new one</li><li>Teach classes for a skill you have</li><li>Recommended 1 hour per week</li></ul>

Community Service Log

Type of service: _____

Date of Service	Service Description	Amount of Time Served	Person and/or Agency Signature	Parent/ Guardian Signature
Week 1				
Week 2				
Week 3				
Week 4				
Week 5				
Week 6				
Week 7				
Week 8				
Week 9				
Week 10				

Empathy

TOOL 1: EMPATHY INTERVIEW (FOUR-STEP PROCESS)

Process: What is an empathy interview? To understand the experience(s) of the user (i.e., student), you have to allow for a safe opportunity for students to share their thoughts, emotions, experiences, and motivations to help meet their social and emotional needs.

- **Step 1: Introductions**. Introduce yourself/role (e.g., teacher, counselor, admin), and have the student introduce themselves.

- **Step 2: Purpose**. Explain the purpose of the interview/check-in to the student, and let them know their input is valued.

  Tip: Actively listen to the student and be authentic.

- **Step 3: Questions.** Ask neutral questions.

  Tip: Avoid asking binary questions that can be answered in a word. Ask, "Why?" Pay attention to nonverbal cues and observe body language and emotions.

Sample Questions

1. Tell me about your experience(s) in the virtual learning environment.
2. Tell me about your overall virtual learning experience(s).
3. Tell me about the last virtual learning class session(s) you experienced (i.e., encourage stories).
4. What do you feel about your teacher's interaction with you in the virtual learning environment?
5. Why do you feel that way? Is there anything else you would like to share?

- **Step 4: Wrap Up.** Thank them, wrap up, validate their input, and set up a follow-up to share the actions taken based on their input.

Empathy Interview (Four-Step Process) Template

Cautionary note: Use this as a guide and template, not as a script. Empathy interviews should be conversational to build rapport. Verbatim note-taking to each question will break rapport and create an inauthentic experience.

Interview date: _____

Interviewer: _____

Interviewee: _____

Step 1: Introductions. Introduce yourself/role (e.g., teacher, counselor, administrator) and have the student introduce themselves.

> *Write notes about the interviewee here:*

Step 2: Purpose. Explain the purpose of the interview/check-in to the student and let them know their input is valued.

> *Did I explain the purpose of this interview/check-in? YES or NO*
>
> *Did the student have any questions? If so, note them here:*

Step 3: Questions. Sample questions: Tell me about your experience(s) in the virtual learning environment. What do you feel about your teacher's interaction with you in the virtual learning environment? Why? Is there anything else you would like to share?

> *Log the question(s) asked and response(s) below:*
>
> *Question posed:*
>
> *Interviewee response:*
>
> *Question posed:*
>
> *Interviewee response:*
>
> *Question posed:*
>
> *Interviewee response:*
>
> *Question posed:*
>
> *Interviewee response:*

Step 4: Wrap Up. Thank them, wrap up, validate their input, and set up a follow-up to share the actions taken as a result of their input.

> *Did you thank them? YES or NO*
>
> *Did you validate their input? Restate the trends from their responses and write them below to make sure you heard what the interviewee was saying.*
>
> *Validation statements:*
>
> *I heard you share . . .*
>
> *I heard you share . . .*
>
> *I heard you share . . .*
>
> *Schedule a follow-up interview to share the actions taken as a result of their input. Follow-up interview date: _____*

Note: You can also teach students how to conduct empathy interviews, student-to-student, or student-to-a-community-member interviews.

Appreciating Diversity

TOOL 1: #STUDENTSTORY

Process: Give students an opportunity to develop and post about themselves, their perspectives, or their passions using the hashtag #StudentStory. You can do so in a safe and respectful manner in multiple ways, but a simple one is creating a joint classroom PowerPoint and having a slide for each student. After students complete their slide, the slide show can be viewed as a class. Students can insert questions or comments next to slides based on what group they are in for discussion. This will give students the opportunity to learn about the diversity among them all and appreciate them by having a healthy dialogue.

#StudentStory Template
Your name: _____
Insert favorite photo of yourself
Write a status update about yourself

Note: Give students opportunities in small groups to comment or ask questions.

TOOL 2: SPEED MEETINGS (2 MINUTES × FIVE DIFFERENT STUDENTS)

Process: Assign reading, video, and so on prior to class on diverse topics based on student interests, research, and input. Set up speed meetings for students to discuss what they learned from the reading or video. Prior to beginning this process, review classroom norms of respecting diverse reflections and perspectives. Survey students to find topics they are passionate about or that they would like to learn more about. Have students research readings, videos, or similar related to the topic they are interested in navigating through as a class. Once topics and readings are chosen, make sure to allow time for students to read or watch the video.

Set up 2-minute meetings each with five different students. For the speed meetings, first, one student shares for a minute, while the other student is taking notes and listening, and then the other student shares for a minute their key learnings or perspectives, while the other student is taking notes and listening. Have the students reflect using a tool like the one below.

Topic	Reading/video	What I learned from the reading, video, etc.	What I learned from my discussions with other classmates considering their diverse perspectives on this topic

TOOL 3: LEARN SOMETHING NEW ABOUT OR FROM OUR COMMUNITY

Process: Have a guest speaker come in and share what they do in the community. Give students an opportunity to ask the guest questions and write them a class thank you afterward. Students can provide some names of organizations in the community they want to learn about and draft and help with the process of bringing in community members to speak to the class. What follows is a sample letter.

Dear Community Member,

We would love for you to speak to our class about your [organization, business, etc.]. If you are willing to virtually visit our classroom, we will be in contact soon and work out a day and time that works best for you. Thank you in advance.

Sincerely,
Mrs. Hannigan's class

Respect for Others

TOOL 1: VIRTUAL CLASSROOM AGREEMENTS

Process:

- **Step 1:** Review the SOAR Virtual Agreement with students (Figure 7, page 83).
- **Step 2:** Tell students you want their voice and agreement as to what this should look like in your classroom.
- **Step 3:** As a class or in groups, have students list as positive statements what they agree to in each quadrant.
- **Step 4:** Have a discussion and consensus for each quadrant.
- **Step 5:** Have students sign the agreement (virtually sign).
- **Step 6:** Review the virtual agreement every week.
- **Step 7:** Virtual learning agreement check-in and adjust. (Create poll: How did we do?)

<table>
<tr><td colspan="3" align="center">Sample SOAR Virtual Agreement
(Self-control, On-task, Achievement, and Respect)</td></tr>
<tr>
<td>

Students-to-Students Demonstrating SOAR
- Avoid distractions
- Allow for different opinions
- Work together
- Communicate kindly

</td>
<td>

Students-to-Teacher Demonstrating SOAR
- Listen and ask questions for clarity
- Be on time
- Come prepared

</td>
<td rowspan="2">

Mr. Hannigan's Period 4 Student Electronic Signatures

Jessica

John

Henry

Matt

Veronica

Jesus

Damien

M-wasi

Angel

Frank

Riley

Rowan

JJ

Matt

Andrew

Martina

</td>
</tr>
<tr>
<td>

Teacher-to-Students Demonstrating SOAR
- Limit busy work
- Be understanding
- Assume best intentions
- Treat us fairly

</td>
<td>

Everyone-to-Virtual-Learning-Environment Demonstrating SOAR
- Stay on task
- Use kind words
- Be engaged

</td>
</tr>
</table>

TOOL 2: VIRTUAL CLASSROOM AGREEMENT MONITORING FORM

Process: Use the Virtual Classroom Agreement Monitoring Form to progress monitor how the class is doing with their classroom agreements. For example, if there is an area that needs extra focus, the class can discuss it and collectively rate how they think they are doing toward implementing their agreement. If the goal is not met, the class can determine collectively what they need to do to move up to the higher rating. At least once a month, the classroom agreement should be reviewed for progress.

Note: This can also be utilized with a small group of students who are not responding to the agreement and need reteaching and monitoring opportunities.

Virtual Classroom Agreement Monitoring Form

Class: _____   Date: _____

Top Classroom Behaviors: How did we do?	Previous Week:
	Circle one: Good Fair Poor
	Circle one: Good Fair Poor

What worked for us?

What didn't work for us?

Contract for this week:

We _____ will work on _____ this week to meet our classroom behavior goal.

Classroom or Student Group Designee Signature: _____

Teacher Signature: _____

TOOL 3: SEL DAILY LESSON TEMPLATE

Process: Use the SEL Daily Lesson Template to make sure multiple teaching modalities are embedded in your daily lesson focus. Use the template to cross-check your lesson. It can also be used for students to help create their own lessons. You can give them a focus area and have them work through how they would teach the identified skill. You can even have them record themselves teaching or explaining their lesson. This recording can be used for younger grades, to teach your class (students own their learning), or to provide additional ideas to other teachers.

SEL Daily Lesson Template
Skill
Introduction and Rationale
Teacher Model
Role-play *Example:* *Non-example:* *Example:* *Student Example:*
Review
Practice Throughout the Day
Homework
Supplemental Activities

TOOL 4: "SHOWING RESPECT" FORM

Process: You can have students independently complete this form, or you can complete it with them as a class. You can do a poster contest or have students share and describe their posters in small groups or as a whole class.

"Showing Respect" Template
Write a plan on how you show respect:
What could happen when you do not show respect to others?
What makes you someone who is respectful?
Write three classroom rules that help everyone act respectfully.
What consequences should be in place for students who do not show respect?
Give some examples of things that **do** demonstrate respect and examples that **do not** demonstrate respect:
_____   _____   _____   _____   _____   _____   _____   _____   _____   _____
On the back of this page, make a poster about being respectful. (*Note:* You can make a poster in a virtual setting using Word drawing features or by inserting images.)

TOOL 5: SOAR VIRTUAL LEARNING MATRIX

Process: For each bulleted item and each behavior expectation in Figure 7, students need to be taught what is expected of them. They also need to hear consistent language and have the structure in place to ensure they are learning in a safe environment. You can post this figure in your virtual classroom, have it as the first slide of a lesson, include it in your emails or class webpage, or use it as a wallpaper background while you are teaching. Use the Matrix as a guide to make sure students understand what is expected of them in the virtual classroom environment. There are many ways you can use this as a teaching tool with the students: Review the Matrix with students prior to synchronous instruction, have them provide examples of the wrong and right ways for each bullet item as a warm-up, have students develop tips for demonstrating the appropriate behaviors in small groups, or have them come up with creative ways to remember the expectations (e.g., create videos). For older students, it could be reviewed as part of the syllabus and discussed in conversation as a whole class or in small groups based on areas that are not being demonstrated by students in the classroom.

Figure 7

SOAR Virtual Learning Matrix

S
SELF-CONTROL

→

- Follow instructions
- Wait for your turn to speak or contribute
- Use the raise-your-hand feature
- Minimize distractions
- Utilize chat features appropriately

O
ON-TASK

→

- Log in on time
- Be present/actively engaged
- Organize your materials
- Set daily goals
- Make yourself visible
- Have a backup plan if you get disconnected

A
ACHIEVEMENT

→

- Complete tasks on time/stay on top of assignments
- Be prepared
- Complete preparation work
- Reach out to the teacher for help
- Share and collaborate
- Write in complete sentences
- Create a schedule/space to complete assignments

R
RESPECT

→

- Mute microphone when others are speaking
- Respect others' perspectives
- Use kind words
- Use proper text etiquette
- Help each other during group assignments and in designated meeting rooms
- Resolve conflict peacefully

TOOL 6: SOCIAL MEDIA EXERCISE AND PLEDGE

Process: As a class, review each item on this exercise, and pledge and commit to it.

Social Media Exercise and Pledge

What is the purpose of social media (Facebook, Twitter, Instagram, etc.)?

What is cyberbullying?

Are bullying and making inappropriate comments on social media against the law?

Do your messages or pictures disappear when you delete them?

What are five things you are committed to doing to make sure no cyberbullying is happening?

1.
2.
3.
4.
5.

I pledge to do my part to stop cyberbullying. I pledge to always think before I post a message or picture that can hurt myself or others. I also pledge to help a friend by notifying an adult or the school if they are being cyberbullied.

Rewrite the pledge:

Signature: _____ Date: _____

You have reached the end of Social Awareness SEL competency chapter. Now may be a good time to pause and see if you can capture some of the tools and processes aligned with the priority SEL competency you identified at the beginning of this book. In addition, if you need a reference, see a completed template in Chapter 8 on page 122.

SEL From a Distance Planning Template				
SEL Competency Focus:				
SEL Competency Deconstructed Skill:				
This week's mastery evidence (how will you know if your students have mastered the skill?):				
Week of:				
Monday	**Tuesday**	**Wednesday**	**Thursday**	**Friday**
Identify	Identify	Identify	Identify	Identify
Teach	Teach	Teach	Teach	Teach
Model	Model	Model	Model	Model
Reinforce	Reinforce	Reinforce	Reinforce	Reinforce

SELF-MANAGEMENT TOOLS AND PROCESSES

In this chapter, you will find the social and emotional learning (SEL) competency definition of Self-Management, the deconstructed components necessary for mastering this SEL competency, and tools and processes for each. Although we have provided here some of our most effective SEL tools and processes, you can adjust, add to, or refine them with other tools. Remember, the goal is to go beyond just a tool to an intentional process that requires you to *identify, teach, model,* and *reinforce* the SEL skills students need for success in school and in life.

SEL Competency: Self-Management

What is self-management? It is the ability to successfully regulate one's emotions, thoughts, and behaviors in different situations (i.e., effectively managing stress, controlling impulses, and motivating oneself). It is the ability to set and work toward personal and academic goals (see casel.org).

Simply put, we want our students to have the skills they need to recognize their triggers, learn how to regulate emotions, and set, monitor, and follow through on short- and long-term goals. This SEL competency is deconstructed to capture these goals by the following skills:

SEL competency deconstructed skills: Impulse control, stress management, self-discipline, self-motivation, goal setting, organizational skills

In this section, we have provided you with a tool and process for each of the deconstructed skills required for effective mastery of the SEL competency Self-Management.

Note: Although you are seeing the distance learning examples of these tools and processes, it does not mean they cannot be converted to in-person or hybrid settings as well. The way to look at it is this; if you can do it from a distance, you can do it in person or in a hybrid setting as well.

Menu of Tools and Processes for the SEL Competency

SELF-MANAGEMENT

- ☐ Impulse control
- ☐ Stress management
- ☐ Self-discipline
- ☐ Self-motivation
- ☐ Goal setting
- ☐ Organizational skills

Impulse Control

TOOL 1: VIRTUAL BEHAVIOR CONTRACT

Process: This Behavior Contract can be utilized for individual students who are not responding to Tier 1 classroom prevention rules/expectations alone. This tool can also be used for an additional reteaching (Tier 2) opportunity for students who need to focus on one or two areas at a time and reinforced for meeting their goals.

Note: In this sample, you see an array of focus behaviors for your reference, but the best recommendation is to focus on one or two behaviors at a time.

Make sure you talk to students about this contract and that they know what they need to demonstrate to meet their daily goals. It is also powerful if a parent or caregiver can help reinforce the goals. You can create this in Google forms and share it with the student and parent/caregiver daily.

Daily Behavior Contract (ZOOM, Microsoft Teams, Google Meet, etc.)

Date: _____

Student Name: _____

Log-on time

:)	:|	:(
Awesome!	Close, but not yet!	Today isn't what I wanted, tomorrow will be better!

Stay on task

:)	:|	:(
Awesome!	Close, but not yet!	Today isn't what I wanted, tomorrow will be better!

(Continued)

(Continued)

Use features appropriately

Awesome!

Close, but not yet!

Today isn't what I wanted, tomorrow will be better!

Show respect

Awesome!

Close, but not yet!

Today isn't what I wanted, tomorrow will be better!

Speak when called on

Awesome!

Close, but not yet!

Today isn't what I wanted, tomorrow will be better!

Complete assignments

Awesome!

Close, but not yet!

Today isn't what I wanted, tomorrow will be better!

Daily goal met

Awesome!

Close, but not yet!

Today isn't what I wanted, tomorrow will be better!

Images source: istock.com/ctermit.

Note: For older students, instead of faces, you can insert 2, 1, and 0 points as you are creating your contract.

Sample Complete Assignments

Awesome!   (2 points)

Close, but not yet!   (1 point)

Today isn't what I wanted, tomorrow will be better!   (0 point)

Sample Student Contract

Student: _____

Focus SEL skill: _____

Goal: _____

	Mon	**Tues**	**Wed**	**Thurs**	**Fri**
A.M. to Recess					
Recess to Lunch					
Lunch and Lunch Recess					
After-Lunch Recess to the End of School					

_____ ☺'s = Daily Reward _____

_____ ☺'s = Friday Reward _____

Parent's Signature: _____ **Date:** _____

Images source: istock.com/ctermit.

Stress Management

TOOL 1: CIRCLE OF CONTROL EXERCISE

Process: Show the circle to your students and explain that the larger circle is all the things they cannot control, and the inner circle is all the things they can control. You can email a copy or share a copy with the students so they can write on it individually or annotate on the document as a class. The teacher can provide a topic such as stressed-out with online schoolwork.

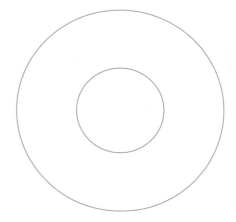

I cannot control . . . , so I will let go of these things by . . .

I can control . . . , so I will focus on these things by . . .

If I need help, I will . . .

· ·

TOOL 2: CLASS STRESS PULSE CHECK-IN

Process:

- **Step 1:** Explain common emotions related to feeling stressed. They set it up as a poster or on a slide (daily check).

- **Step 2:** Through a poll, students will identify how stressed they are feeling.

> How stressed are you feeling as a class today?
>
> **Option 1:** Not stressed at all
>
> **Option 2:** Sort of stressed
>
> **Option 3:** Very stressed

- **Step 3:** Discuss as a class the class rating and next steps.

TOOL 3: VIRTUAL BREAK ROOM

Process: Set up a virtual break room (by individual student) as you are setting up your online instruction for the day. For example, if you have two students who often utilize or need a break room, set up Break Room 1 and Break Room 2 so they have their individual set break room and their own slide link for their break room. If you have certain students you have talked to about using a break appropriately when they are feeling stressed or overwhelmed, they can message you or show you a signal on their image (decided together) and be moved to their designated break room for a set amount of time. There they can practice their stress management strategies and use their break room slide deck as an ongoing resource (individual student break room slide deck link can be created by you and sent to the student privately as they are being sent to the break room). If you are able, it would be nice if you could check in on the students to see how they are doing. In the break room, students can be allowed to play music or pull up a picture that is calming to them. Ultimately, the goal is that students can monitor their own stress levels, use the breaks appropriately, and come back into the virtual learning environment.

Note: If a student is misusing the break room option or is excessively needing to use it, it is probably best to collaborate with the student and, if appropriate, the parent/caregiver about additional supports.

You can have a slide in the virtual break room, or students can pull up the slides with a predesignated link to have prompts for the students. The following are some sample deck prompts.

Note: These can be set ahead of time with individual students too, so they can get to a place where they can pull it up and view or listen as they are in the room.

Sample Deck Prompts

Slide 1: Welcome to the break room (remember, this is a set time for you to practice your strategies so you can return back to class).

Slide 2: What were you feeling before asking to go to the break room?
What is one strategy you will practice during this time? _____

Slide 3: Insert a picture or play a song that calms you down (insert the link to the song), so you will have it there the next time you ask for a break.

Self-Discipline

TOOL 1: SELF-MONITORING FORM
(OLDER AND YOUNGER STUDENT VERSIONS)

Process: Teach students how to identify priorities for the week and set up a time during daily instruction to self-monitor the progress on priority tasks. Walk students through the prompts as a whole class for the first few weeks to help them think about the reasons that have impacted their completion of priority tasks.

Self-Monitoring Form for Older Students

Student Name: _____   Week of: _____

This week's priority: tasks/ assignments/ projects, etc. and due date	I completed on time (explain what strategy helped you complete on time)	I completed late (explain what made you late)	I did not complete it (explain why you did not complete and what your plan is to complete)
1.			
2.			
3.			
4.			
5.			

Monday:	Tuesday:	Wednesday:	Thursday:	Friday:
Teacher initials:	Teacher initials:	Teacher initials:	Teacher initials:	Teacher initials:
Student initials:	Student initials:	Student initials:	Student initials:	Student initials:

Self-Monitoring Form for Younger Students

Student Name: _____   Week of: _____

This week's priority	I completed on time (explain what strategy helped you complete on time) ☺	I completed late (explain what made you late) 😐	I did not complete (explain why you did not complete and what your plan is to complete) ☹
1.			
2.			
3.			
4.			
5.			

Monday:	Tuesday:	Wednesday:	Thursday:	Friday:
Teacher initials:	Teacher initials:	Teacher initials:	Teacher initials:	Teacher initials:
Student initials:	Student initials:	Student initials:	Student initials:	Student initials:

Images source: istock.com/ctermit.

Self-Motivation

TOOL 1: PASSION PROJECT PROPOSAL

Process: Allow students to propose a passion project to you. Have them develop their passion project assignment and their best learning modality for that passion area. Have students present their proposals to you individually or in small groups; adjust as needed and set a realistic due date for the students. Set up a passion project sharing week where students get to share their projects in small groups, or even with community members, in a virtual format. *Note:* A good way to set up a structure for passion projects is to designate time for students to work on them while you are doing individual checks-in on their progress. You can also create a timeline for completion with check-in dates via email or individual student meetings.

Passion Project Proposal Template

Passion project topic area:

- Why do you want to pursue this passion project?
- What format is your passion project going to be presented in? (PowerPoint, Prezi, video, paper, voice-over, etc.)
- How is this project relevant to your learning?
- How is this project meaningful to you?

TOOL 2: ACTION BEFORE MOTIVATION (A-BEFORE-M) CHALLENGE

Process: Talk with students about motivation. Sometimes it will come after a series of small wins. Share with them that 10 days of small wins equals a new habit. Ask them to identify something they have always wanted to be better at but do not feel motivated to do so. Have them identify a small step they will take toward that goal. Do a daily check with the students in the morning and remind them of the A-Before-M Challenge.

Action Before Motivation

New positive habit goal:

- What is a small step I can take each day for the next 10 days toward that goal?

Note: Please let the student know it is okay if they miss a day, and to start over the next day toward their 10-days-in-a-row habit goal. Mark "Yes" or "No" for each day.

How did I do?

Day 1	Day 2	Day 3	Day 4	Day 5	Day 6	Day 7	Day 8	Day 9	Day 10

TOOL 3: SELF-MOTIVATION CHECK

Process: Show the Self-Motivation Check on your screen and allow a student or students to read the statements independently, or you can can read each statement and explain what it means. Answer any clarifying questions about the statements. Students can then drag the check marks to their self-motivation rating for each statement. This can be done in Google slides every day. You can work with the students to focus on at least one area of the Self-Motivation Check rating each week: The area can be a classroom goal based on how the class responded, or students can have individual goals based on their self-rating.

Self-Motivation Check	
Let's check in with your motivation today.	
Yes ✓ Working on it ✓ Not yet ✓	
I work hard to achieve my goals.	
I meet my deadlines I set for myself.	
I am able to bounce back quickly if something interrupts me from achieving my goals.	
I put in full effort in achieving my goals.	
I believe if I work hard and apply myself, I will achieve my goals.	
I push myself to get assignments done.	
I'm sure of my ability to achieve the goals I set for myself.	
I regularly set goals and achieve them.	
I set up my environment for success in meeting my goals.	

Goal Setting

TOOL 1: WEEKLY GOAL-SETTING SHEET

Process: Talk with students about the areas necessary for successful goal setting. Have students complete this form at the start of the week: (1) prioritize goals (goals can be personal or school focused), (2) visualize a target, and (3) set a date. Provide time for students to discuss progress on their goals with you. Allow for an hour to sign up students who need additional support in setting and meeting their goals.

Prioritize goals (list)	Visualize a target	Set a date	Did I meet my goal?
☐ Little Things (start tomorrow) ☐ Key Moves (3–6 months) ☐ Big Plays (6–9 months)	☐ Two things that I need to accomplish ☐ Two things that I need to avoid		
Sample: *Goal 1 (Little Things): Logging in on time all week*	**Sample:** *Accomplish:* • *Waking up 10 minutes earlier using my phone alarm and going to bed earlier* *Avoid:* • *Staying up all night playing video games or staying up all night watching TikToks*	**Sample:** *By the end of the week (Friday—will review if 5 out of 5 days)*	**Sample:** *Yes—met my goal of logging in on time to class all week*

TOOL 2: PORTRAIT OF A STUDENT

Process: Speak with students about the importance of both short-term and long-term goal setting. Have them think about a portrait of a successful student in your class, grade level, or aligned with the school mascot (or even a portrait of a graduate for high schoolers). At first, reflect on each of these areas as a class so students can start thinking about some ideas for self, others, and community. You can create a portrait together as a class, or you can assign students to create individual portraits and maybe add on to the classroom one to make it unique for themselves. These portraits can be utilized as goal-monitoring talking points with you throughout the school year or semester.

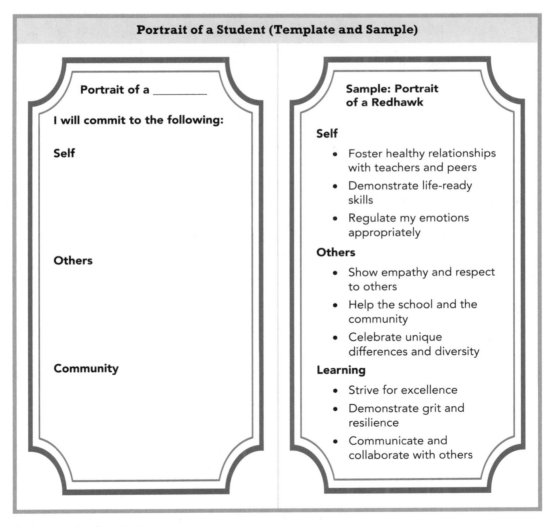

Portrait of a Student (Template and Sample)

Portrait of a _____

I will commit to the following:

Self

Others

Community

Sample: Portrait of a Redhawk

Self
- Foster healthy relationships with teachers and peers
- Demonstrate life-ready skills
- Regulate my emotions appropriately

Others
- Show empathy and respect to others
- Help the school and the community
- Celebrate unique differences and diversity

Learning
- Strive for excellence
- Demonstrate grit and resilience
- Communicate and collaborate with others

Border source: istock.com/amtitus.

Organizational Skills

TOOL 1: PRIORITIZING ORGANIZER

Process: Set an organization check time (How are we doing, and what do we need?). Conduct a class poll to see how organized students are feeling overall with their classroom assignments and workload.

Poll Prompt
On a scale of 1 (not organized at all) to 5 (very organized):   • Have students share why they rated themselves in the "not organized at all range" and request suggestions for how to help them.   • Have students who rated in the very organized range share examples of what strategies they are using to stay organized.   • Have all students create two lists independently and give them a designated time to check off or add items to their list each day of the week.   • Set up a minute check-in with each student while others are working on an independent assignment.

Write down this week's 1. **Short-term goals** 2. **Smaller assignments or projects due this week**	**Write down this month's** 1. **Long-term goals** 2. **Larger assignments and group projects due at the end of the month**
☐ Priority 1:	☐ Priority 1:
☐ Priority 2:	☐ Priority 2:
☐ Priority 3:	☐ Priority 3:

You have reached the end of the Self-Management SEL competency chapter. Now may be a good time to pause and see if you can capture some of the tools and processes aligned with the priority SEL competency you identified at the beginning of this book. In addition, if you need a reference, see a completed template in Chapter 8 on page 122.

SEL From a Distance Planning Template

SEL Competency Focus:

SEL Competency Deconstructed Skill:

This week's mastery evidence (how will you know if your students have mastered the skill?):

Week of:

Monday	Tuesday	Wednesday	Thursday	Friday
Identify	Identify	Identify	Identify	Identify
Teach	Teach	Teach	Teach	Teach
Model	Model	Model	Model	Model
Reinforce	Reinforce	Reinforce	Reinforce	Reinforce

SELF-AWARENESS TOOLS AND PROCESSES

CHAPTER

7

In this chapter, you will find the social and emotional learning (SEL) competency definition of Self-Awareness, the deconstructed components necessary for mastering this SEL competency, and tools and processes for each. Although we provided some of our most effective SEL tools and processes here, you can adjust, add to, or refine them with other tools as well. Remember, the goal is to go beyond just a tool to an intentional process that requires you to *identify, teach, model,* and *reinforce* the SEL skills students need for success in school and in life.

SEL Competency: Self-Awareness

What is self-awareness? It is the ability to accurately recognize one's own emotions, thoughts, and values, and how they influence behavior. In addition, it is the ability to accurately assess one's strengths and limitations, with a well-grounded sense of confidence, optimism, and a growth mindset (see casel.org).

Simply put, we want our students to have the skills they need to recognize their gifts and qualities, develop a positive self-image, and respect themselves and others. This SEL competency is deconstructed to capture these goals by the following skills:

SEL competency deconstructed skills: Identifying emotions, accurate self-perception, recognizing strengths, self-confidence, and self-efficacy

In this section, we have provided you with a tool and process for each of the deconstructed skills required for effective mastery of the SEL competency Self-Awareness.

Note: Although you are seeing the distance learning examples of these tools and processes, it does not mean they cannot be converted to in-person or hybrid settings. The way to look at it is this: If you can do it from a distance, you can do it in person or in a hybrid setting as well.

Menu of Tools and Processes for the SEL Competency

SELF-AWARENESS

- ☐ Identifying emotions
- ☐ Accurate self-perception
- ☐ Recognizing strengths
- ☐ Self-confidence
- ☐ Self-efficacy

Identifying Emotions

TOOL 1: DAILY SEL CHECK-IN

Process: Create a class SEL check-in poll or Google form (set it as anonymous) so that you can quickly and privately take the pulse of your class. You can even create a word map with responses from students. For each of these areas ("We feel . . ." and "We need to . . ."), have the students follow the same process individually with an "I feel . . ." or "I need to . . ." prompt.

How do we feel overall as a class?	
We feel . . . • Overwhelmed • Open-minded • Stressed • Included • Disorganized • Relaxed • Sad • Energized • Happy • Proud • Upset • Scared • Alone • Worried • Angry • Tired • Anxious • Calm	**We need to . . .**

How do I feel?	
I feel . . . (circle one or two) • Overwhelmed • Open-minded • Stressed • Included • Disorganized • Relaxed • Sad • Energized • Happy • Proud • Upset • Scared • Alone • Worried • Angry • Tired • Anxious • Calm	**I need to . . .**

TOOL 2: VIRTUAL MINDFULNESS MINUTES

Process:

- **Step 1: Imagery.** Talk to students about the importance of practicing mindfulness: being in the moment, accepting their feelings, focusing on themselves. Tell them you will insert mindfulness minutes every hour of virtual instruction or whatever your preference may be (set reminders or designate a student to remind you when it is time to practice). Decide on a mindfulness image or music as a class, or have students select their own imagery that helps them focus on themselves (e.g., an image of an ocean can be someone's imagery to cancel out all other noise and focus on accepting feelings). Give them examples.

Feel	See
Hear	Smell
Taste	Touch

- **Step 2: Pause.** Give the mindfulness minutes cue or signal to the students; this signal means everyone pauses what they are doing and practices mindfulness for a designated time, such as 2 minutes. A timer can be up as a visual for students. Students can shut their eyes, shut off their video, and get comfortable before you set the timer.

  Prompts: Take a deep breath break. Breath in through the nose. Breath out through the mouth.

- **Step 3: Validate and Reflect.** After the designated time, students will be thanked and validated for how they feel and practicing mindfulness. You can have students share out what helped them practice mindfulness. In addition, students can write down reflections in a virtual mindfulness journal describing how they felt before and after the mindfulness minutes.

Accurate Self-Perception

TOOL 1: "VIRTUAL CAMERA IMAGERY" EXERCISE

Process: Talk to students about the importance of developing and maintaining a strong positive self-image. Tell them to imagine looking into a mirror or a virtual camera.

Give students the prompt: What is your self-image? Have them list "I am" statements and insert them into the virtual camera space.

- I am . . .
- I am . . .
- I am . . .
- I am . . .
- I am . . .

Remind them to repeat these self-image statements daily. Give students time to reflect on their self-image daily. Remind them that sometimes feelings do not match a self-image (e.g., you might feel really down or frustrated, but that is just what you are feeling in this moment of time, not who you are). Negative feelings can impact our self-image if we let them. "I feel therefore I am" is the wrong way to think about your self-image.

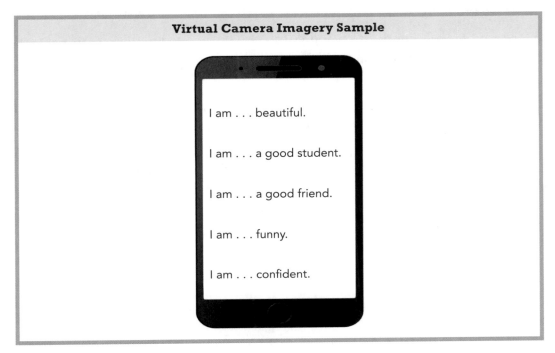

Virtual Camera Imagery Sample

I am . . . beautiful.

I am . . . a good student.

I am . . . a good friend.

I am . . . funny.

I am . . . confident.

Image source: istock.com/Pavlo Stavnichuk.

TOOL 2: EMAIL/LETTER TO SELF

Process: Have students write an email/letter to themselves. Before they do so, tell them to write down some of their insecurities on a piece of paper privately. Have them write for 1 minute. After a minute, have the students crumple or rip up the paper.

Next, tell your students they are going to be writing a self-compliment email/letter to themselves using the template provided.

Letter to Self Template

Dear Self,

   I like . . . about myself.

   I like . . . about myself.

   I like . . . about myself.

   I like . . . about myself.

Sincerely,

_____

Provide an opportunity for sharing if students feel comfortable to do so; if not, just have them send the letter and CC you on the email.

Self-perception tip: One reason students stop their video to avoid showing their faces during a class Zoom session is because they are not comfortable showing the inside of their home or bedroom. A home is a very private and personal place.

When a student isn't sharing their video, one solution could be to provide students with three to five choices of a virtual background of school spirit banner options with the school name and mascot. This will allow the student to maintain privacy *and* show their faces.

Recognizing Strengths

TOOL 1: GROWTH MINDSET EXERCISE

Process: Have students independently complete the growth mindset prompts for themselves.

- About me
- Growth mindset
- I am already good at
- I would like to get better at

Note: For younger students, you can have them draw a picture or use sentence starters to talk about their strengths as superpowers.

- My superpowers . . .
- My superpower is . . .
- My superpower is . . .
- My superpower is . . .
- A new superpower I would love to have is . . .

TOOL 2: SELF-ESTEEM LESSON

Process: Use the steps in this lesson to help students identify their strengths. You can do this as a whole class or in small groups. Follow the partner sharing and writing prompts for students to complete.

Self-Esteem Lesson

Objective: This exercise will help students self-define their self-worth and set up personal criteria for judging self-worth. This exercise will also assist the students in determining gifts and potentials.

Goal: Sometimes it is hard for children to like themselves. Peer pressure, social comparisons, and daily measurement in intellectual, physical, social, and emotional well-being can hurt anyone's self-esteem, and all of these things happen daily. The students need to learn to look at themselves and realize the gifts, talents, and potentials they have and not measure their self-worth in comparison to other people. In other words, students need to learn how to determine their self-worth, and subsequently self-esteem, through self-imposed achievements, expectations, and gifts, not measurements set up by the outside world.

Consequences of not using this skill:	Benefits of using this skill:
Constantly comparing your shortcomings to other people's strengths will result in low self-esteem issues.	Being able to identify and set goals according to your own strengths and talents rather than those of others will enable you to have a healthier perspective of self-worth and self-esteem.

Right Ways and No Ways

Exercise 1: Ask the group to tell if the following is the "right way" or "no way."

- Louie always wanted to be good at baseball, but he's not, so he doesn't try. (No way)
- Rachel wants to learn to play the flute, so she practices every day. (Right way)
- Ronnie doesn't like the way his voice sounds, so he never raises his hand in class. (No way)
- Lucinda doesn't have very good handwriting, so she asks a friend to spend some time showing her what she does to get better. (Right way)

Exercise 2: Have students identify an example of a "right way" and a "no way" with a partner or a group and have them share with the class or in small groups the reasoning for their selections.

Writing Prompts

Select or have students select the prompt that they would like to respond to:

- Why is it important to have goals?
- Why is it important to know the things you are good at?
- Should you work to get better at the things you are already good at?
- Why do people work to make themselves better?

TOOL 3: HELP-SEEKING PROMPTS

Process: Talk to students about the importance of recognizing their own strengths, but also their areas of weakness so they know how to get help when necessary. Provide these short prompts to the students and see if they know the right way and wrong way of seeking help. Have students come up with other scenarios where someone might need help and what they can do to solicit it. Also, provide them with an "I need assistance" link so they have confidentiality when asking the teacher for help if needed.

Help-Seeking Prompts

Wrong way: I do not want or know how to ask for help, so I am just going to get zero points on this assignment. I don't even think my teacher can give me a real grade during this time.

Right way: Take initiative to email the teacher with clarification questions or set up a time to conference with the teacher to get help.

Insert an "I Need Assistance" link on the class webpage or below every email where students can submit a form. This can be done in a Google format or an email format. The idea is that the link is visible, accessible, and students know they are going to get a response from the teacher in a timely and safe fashion.

I Need Assistance

Your name:

What can I help you with?

What is the best way to contact you?

Thank you for trusting me and reaching out. I will help you navigate through this challenge.

Image source: istock.com/-VICTOR-.

Self-Confidence

TOOL 1: CLASSROOM POSITIVE AFFIRMATIONS

Process:

- **Step 1:** Getting organized. Get individual student input first. Poll online or in chat.

- **Step 2:** Discuss as a class the five common affirmations that will be part of the morning affirmation moment.

- **Step 3:** Take time every morning to showcase the affirmations. You can insert them into a PowerPoint or slideshow and play them every morning or every period before starting class.

Sample Classroom Affirmations

- I am capable of anything and everything.
- I am a good student.
- I am a kind friend.
- I am ready for any challenges.
- I am capable of pushing myself.

- I am beautiful.
- I am welcomed.
- I have a voice.
- I belong.
- I am loved.

- **Step 4:** Assign a quick write using this format. Post the affirmations so students can see a graphic organizer for their thoughts: Write down three daily goals and three focus affirmations.

Student Affirmation Form

Three Daily Goals	Three Focus Affirmations
Goal 1:	Affirmation:
Goal 2:	Affirmation:
Goal 3:	Affirmation:

Self-Efficacy

TOOL 1: SEL VOCABULARY DEVELOPMENT INDEX CARD TEMPLATE

Process: Complete the areas on the SEL Vocabulary Development Index Card as a class or in small groups. After completion of the index card, add the completed image to a shared slide deck for the class where all the index cards and commitments can be revisited. You can do this exercise as a whole class, or students can complete and share them individually or with partners. Some vocabulary words connected with self-efficacy are *resilient, confidence, self-motivation, self-belief, spirit*, and *self-assurance*.

SEL Vocabulary Development Index Cards		
Classroom Resilience Goal	**Tasks**	**Resilience Commitments (actions I can practice this week)**
Be prepared and ready with some skills for our future challenges or setbacks	Definition:	
	What can I say?	
	What can I do?	
	An example of resilience is . . .	

TOOL 2: DAILY GRATITUDE CHECK

Process: Model for students a daily gratitude check. Say it out loud. Have students write what they are grateful for. Use the Daily Gratitude Check Form as a class to define and brainstorm ways to show gratitude. Have students individually fill out a Gratitude Check Log. Ask students to share out if they feel comfortable doing so.

Daily Gratitude Check Form					
Define gratitude: Why is having gratitude important? What are ways to show gratitude?					
	Monday	**Tuesday**	**Wednesday**	**Thursday**	**Friday**
What am I grateful for this week?					
What is something I can do to show I am grateful?					

TOOL 3: SCAVENGER HUNT

Process: Let students know they will be engaging in a scavenger hunt. You can add these items in a Google form or other format based on your school platform as an assignment for students to complete. Let students know they can insert a link or image, or type in the responses as they are checking off the items in the scavenger hunt. After the scavenger hunt, have students reflect on what they are grateful for in small groups and share out if they are so inclined.

Note: We provided a gratitude example, but you can use other connected terms for this area using the scavenger hunt model.

Gratitude Scavenger Hunt Items
☐ Review and define the meaning of the word gratitude: _____
☐ Find something that makes you happy: _____
☐ Find something you love listening to: _____
☐ Find something you love looking at: _____
☐ Find something you love watching: _____
☐ Find something that is useful for you: _____
☐ Find something you love eating: _____
☐ Find something that is your favorite color: _____
☐ Find something you love reading: _____
☐ Find something that makes you smile: _____
☐ Find something you are thankful for: _____

You have reached the end of the Self-Awareness SEL competency chapter. Now may be a good time to pause and see if you can capture some of the tools and processes aligned with the priority SEL competency you identified at the beginning of this book. In addition, if you need a reference, see a completed template in Chapter 8 on page 122.

SEL From a Distance Planning Template

SEL Competency Focus:

SEL Competency Deconstructed Skill:

This week's mastery evidence (how will you know if your students have mastered the skill?):

Week of:

Monday	Tuesday	Wednesday	Thursday	Friday
Identify	Identify	Identify	Identify	Identify
Teach	Teach	Teach	Teach	Teach
Model	Model	Model	Model	Model
Reinforce	Reinforce	Reinforce	Reinforce	Reinforce

SEL IN PRACTICE

SEL is not just a curriculum; *it is the intentional identification, teaching, modeling, and reinforcement of the necessary SEL skills for success in school and life.*

BRINGING IT ALL TOGETHER: TEACHER TEAM CASE STUDY SAMPLE

In this chapter, we provide a sample of a teacher team going through the three phases of the SEL Competency Implementation Framework using the tools and processes provided in this book.

Where did this teacher team begin? They identified through the SEL Competency Priority Forced Rating Scale a need to focus on the SEL competency Self-Management, especially due to abrupt

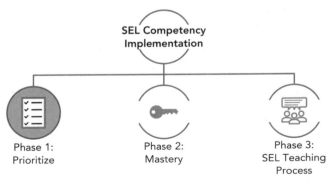

SEL Competency Implementation

Phase 1: Prioritize

Phase 2: Mastery

Phase 3: SEL Teaching Process

distance-learning needs. Based on the rating and additional stakeholder input collected, it was identified that students needed help with self-discipline skills. The teachers and students concluded that students were struggling to self-manage their time, meet their goals, and turn in assignments in the virtual learning environment.

Here is a sample of a completed SEL Competency Priority Forced Rating Scale for this school.

Sample Completed SEL Competency Priority Forced Rating Scale					
Date: *9-1-20*					
Team or individual completing the rating scale: *Sixth-grade teacher team (four members on the team)*					
TM = team member					
SEL Competency	**TM1**	**TM2**	**TM3**	**TM4**	**Overall rank order score** (1 highest priority – 5 lowest priority)
Relationship Skills (i.e., communication, social engagement, relationship building, teamwork)	*4*	*5*	*5*	*5*	*19*
Responsible Decision Making (i.e., identifying problems, analyzing situations, solving problems, evaluation, reflecting, ethical responsibility)	*2*	*2*	*4*	*4*	*12*
Social Awareness (i.e., perspective taking, empathy, appreciating diversity, respect for others)	*3*	*4*	*3*	*3*	*13*
Self-Management (i.e., impulse control, stress management, self-discipline, self-motivation, goal setting, organizational skills)	*1*	*1*	*2*	*1*	*5*
Self-Awareness (i.e., identifying emotions, accurate self-perception, recognizing strengths, self-confidence, self-efficacy)	*5*	*3*	*1*	*2*	*11*
Highest priority SEL competency: *Self-Management (want to begin focus on self-discipline skill)*					

Based on this information, they developed a precise problem statement: *All teachers on this teacher team were reporting a significant decrease in the number of students completing and turning in tasks and assignments on time individually and in groups. Compared to prior to COVID-19 (average 80% of students were completing tasks/ assignments on time), it has decreased to an average of 50% of students in April and May.*

☐ SEL Competency (self-management with the focus on self-discipline skills to address, e.g., struggling with self-monitoring, completing tasks on time, goal setting).

To address these areas with their students through the virtual learning modality, they used the tools and processes in this book to plan in grade-level teams. Use this school as a contextual reference of how to apply the ideas in this book into a classroom setting.

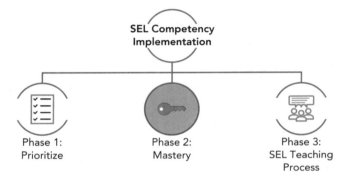

Next the teachers completed a rubric to help identify mastery of this identified skill. See completed sample below.

Sample Completed Rubric for Self-Management (Self-Discipline Skill)			
SEL Competency	**Internalized Mastery** Student independently demonstrates (2)	**Emergent Mastery** Student demonstrates with prompt or cue (1)	**Minimal to No Mastery** Student inconsistently demonstrates or does not demonstrate (0)
Self-Management (Self-Discipline)	*Completes weekly assignments and turns them in on time on the due date independently with no prompt or cue needed*	*Completes weekly assignments and turns them in on time on the due date or 1 day late with multiple reminder prompts and cues*	*Does not complete weekly assignments and does not turn them in on time on the due date, even with multiple prompts and cues*

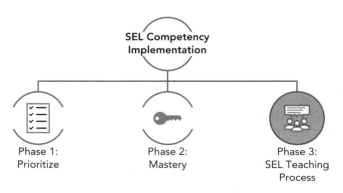

SEL Competency
Implementation

Phase 1:
Prioritize

Phase 2:
Mastery

Phase 3:
SEL Teaching
Process

After defining mastery for their priority, the teacher team used the tools and processes in this book to complete a planning template.

SEL From a Distance Planning Template

SEL Competency Focus: *Self-Management*

SEL Competency Deconstructed Skill: *Self-Discipline*

This week's mastery evidence (how will you know if your students have mastered the skill): *85% of my class will submit work on time and actively participate in joint group assignments/conversations as measured by weekly individual and classroom assignment products.*

Week of: *August 10, 2020*

Monday	Tuesday	Wednesday	Thursday	Friday
Identify: *Self-Discipline*	Identify: *Self-Discipline*	Identify: *Self-Discipline*	Identify: *Self-Discipline*	Identify: *Self-Discipline*
Teach: *Self-Discipline sections of the virtual learning matrix explicitly taught (page 83)*	Teach: *Complete a virtual learning classroom agreement (addressing self-discipline) (page 78)*	Teach: *Introduce and teach students how to use the self-monitoring tool (page 94)*	Teach: *Revisit the self-monitoring tool, show examples (page 94)*	Teach: *Classroom meeting topic (How do we improve classroom self-discipline?) (page 54)*
Model: *Demonstrate self-discipline*	Model: *Include your commitments in the virtual learning classroom agreement*	Model: *Show the students how to use it*	Model: *Highlight how you use it as you plan*	Model: *Actively participate and model steps in classroom meetings*
Reinforce: *Classroom challenge, student voice (develop class weekly goal)*	Reinforce: *Classroom challenge update, verbal praise*	Reinforce: *Classroom challenge update, verbal praise, positive conversations*	Reinforce: *Classroom challenge reminder, highlight students*	Reinforce: *Revisit classroom challenge goal, celebrate growth, and develop new goal (student voice)*

REFERENCES

CASEL.org. (2017). *Social and emotional learning (SEL) competencies.* Retrieved from https://casel.org/wp-content/uploads/2019/12/CASEL-Competencies.pdf

Centers for Disease Control and Prevention & Kaiser Permanente. (2016). *The ACE study survey data* [Unpublished data]. Retrieved from https://www.cdc.gov/violenceprevention/acestudy/fastfact.html

Centers for Disease Control and Prevention. (2020). *Social and emotional climate.* Retrieved from https://www.cdc.gov/healthyschools/sec.htm

Hannigan, J., Hannigan, J. D., Mattos, M., & Buffum, A. (2020). *Behavior solutions: Teaching academic and social skills through RTI at work.* Bloomington, IN: Solution Tree.

Harold, B., & Kurtz, H. Y. (2020). *Teachers work two hours less per day during COVID-19: 8 Key EdWeek survey findings.* Retrieved from https://www.edweek.org/ew/articles/2020/05/11/teachers-work-an-hour-less-per-day.html

Mojtabai, R., Olfson, M., & Han, B. (2016). National trends in the prevalence and treatment of depression in adolescents and young adults. *Pediatrics, 138*(6), e20161878.

National 4-H Council & Harris Poll. (2020). *The state of teen mental health during COVID-19 in America: A 4-H and Harris Poll youth mental health survey.* Retrieved from https://theharrispoll.com/the-state-of-teen-mental-health-during-covid-19-in-america-a-4%E2%80%91h-and-harris-poll-youth-mental-health-survey/

National Institute of Mental Health. (2018). *Statistics*. Retrieved from htpps://www.nimh.nih.gov/health/statistics/index.shtml

Saeki, E., Jimerson, S. R., Earhart, J., Hart, S. R., Renshaw, T., Singh, R. D., & Stewart, K. (2011). Response to intervention (RtI) in the social, emotional, and behavioral domains: Current challenges and emerging possibilities. *Contemporary School Psychology, 15*(1), 43–52.

Skiba, R., & Rausch, M. K. (2006). School disciplinary systems: Alternatives to suspension and expulsion. In G. G. Bear & K. M. Minke (Eds.), *Children's needs III: Development, prevention, and intervention* (pp. 87–102). Bethesda, MD: National Association of School Psychologists.

U.S. Department of Education. (2014). *Guiding principles: A resource guide for improving school climate and discipline.* Washington, DC: Author. Retrieved from www2.ed.gov/policy/gen/guid/school-discipline/guiding-principles.pdf

Visser, S. N., Danielson, M. L., Bitsko, R. H., Holbrook, J. R., Kogan, M. D., Ghandour, R. M., . . . Blumberg, S. J. (2014). Trends in the parent-report of health care provider-diagnosed and medicated attention-deficit/hyperactivity disorder: United States, 2003–2011. *Journal of the American Academy of Child & Adolescent Psychiatry, 53*(1), 34–46.

A SAGE Publishing Company

Helping educators make the greatest impact

CORWIN HAS ONE MISSION: to enhance education through intentional professional learning.

We build long-term relationships with our authors, educators, clients, and associations who partner with us to develop and continuously improve the best evidence-based practices that establish and support lifelong learning.

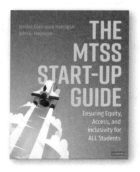
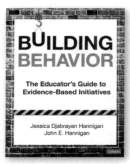

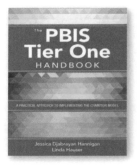